Where is she?

Travel to Trauma: One Woman's Journey to Completely Losing Herself

By Alyshia Ford

Where is she? Travel to Trauma: One Woman's Journey to Completely Losing Herself

Book cover design by Polly Strider
www.freedomstriderstudios.com

Editing and proofreading by Amanda
www.letsgetbooked.com

Formatting by Bojan
www.letsgetbooked.com

ISBN : 9781726319126

Contents

Dedication

For every man, woman and child yet to find a trickle of
light beneath the darkest of skies.

Disclaimer

The story you are about to read, including conversations, and events that took place, have been recreated from my memories. Some names and locations have been changed to protect the innocent— and the not so innocent.

Preface

If you are looking for a book filled with tips and tricks for travelling the world, this story is not for you. The great stretches of the Outback and the high-rise buildings of Melbourne are described only in how my journey shifted because of them. This is my story, the lessons I learnt, the people I met, and the path I took that was forever changing.

Acknowledgements

To my parents, who no matter what, believed in my passions and adventures.

To the friends I made—without you, my travels would have had no colour.

To Scott, who gave my life more than just purpose.

To Sharon—my hero, my saviour, and my friend.

To Daniel, without you, I may never have found the light that kept me searching in the dark. You are my Superman.

To Rita, who let me into her past, her present, and her home. You are beautiful.

To my patrons—without you, this message may never have been heard.

To my viewers—without even knowing, you gave me hope.

Prologue

A deep rhythmic thumping sounds against my ears as I stare wide-eyed at the pale wooden gate at the back of the pub.

Don't make me go in there again.

His blue uniformed sleeve stretches over the gate pulling the bolt that was preventing us from entering. I slowly enter the garden area, my eyes darting rapidly from side to side as I wring my hands together.

I lift my tired leg up to the first step of the building, praying that it will be empty, that I can run upstairs. Stepping close to the silver wall of the cold-room, figures I recognise appear in the kitchen to my left. Eyes straight. Keep going.

My pace increases as I hurtle towards the staircase to get to my room.

'I'm just going to talk to Karen and Robert, OK?' the man in blue said, stopping me in my tracks at the bottom of the stairs.

I nod, keep my head down and dart into my room, quietly closing the door behind me and locking it shut. I perch slightly on the edge of my bed, wrapping my arms around my waist in an attempt to slow my shaking body.

Where Is She?

Creeping along the hallway towards the bathroom, I quickly lock myself into the shower cubical. The cold shards of water hit my body like daggers as I stand under the silver faucet, attempting to rid myself of the past twelve hours.

My eyes refuse to close as my wet hair soaks the pillow beneath my head.

The room is suddenly dark as I lift myself up from an empty sleep. I scramble for my phone under my pillow and wait for Scott to answer.

I cry hysterically, begging for him to save me. I cannot recall the rest of our conversation.

'Karen is here, do you want to speak to her?' Emily's soft voice speaks from the other side of the door.

Cautiously pulling the door towards me, I see Karen; she is waiting anxiously for me to speak. I step towards her and fall into her arms, stifling a sob. She leads me down the corridor towards her part of the building and sits me down on the sofa next to her.

'You have to tell me who did this, Aly. You know you do. I can't put you back behind that bar when it's a local who did this,' Karen insists, as she moves closer to me.

My mind is spinning, trying to figure out how to disappear. Is magic real? Could I vanish into thin air and float away from everything?

'The police couldn't tell me, so you have to. Come on Aly, who was it?'

My head spins faster as I wring my hands together forcefully, wishing I could wake up from this nightmare. I take a long, deep exhale as the words slip out of my mouth.

'You sold the pub to him.'

Horror flashes across her face. And at that moment, her world joins mine in the rubble and ash that surrounds our feet.

PART ONE

Chapter One

Mom, Dad. I Think I'm a Traveller.

It's 2am one early blustering October morning in Birmingham. I awaken to my father's voice whispering, 'It's time to go on holiday!' My seven-year-old self leaps from the covers, a grin plastered across my face. The taxi is pre-booked. Our suitcases are crammed. Bacon and sausage were stuffed in at the last minute, my parents couldn't stand the foreign brands. Four hours early to the airport. The same game every year. Everything waiting for us on arrival. Transfers. Places to go. Nice resort. Swimming pool. Cool apartment.

-Seventeen years later.

It's 3.30am one early, warm November morning in Bali. I wake with a wretched hangover and a growling stomach, battling out the mix of Long Island ice teas and Balinese food. I flop out of bed and wander aimlessly, rolling and throwing things into my backpack. Free hotel essentials are crammed into the top of my pack at the last minute. I make a mental note of what I would need to declare on re-entering Australia. Hours early to the airport. Bank balance once again running low. Cheap room booked in Perth the night previous. Don't know what it will be like. Don't know how we will get there. Don't know what's next. Coffee. Cigarette. Take-off.

Dr. Alyshia Ford. Three words that ran through my head for the entirety of my final year at university. The stepping blocks from undergraduate psychology to clinical doctorate were not simple. I was under no illusion about how difficult and time consuming it is to climb the ladder. First, your three years at university learning the basics. A master's degree perhaps in your chosen field. Multiple years as an assistant psychologist. Applications to get on a clinical psychology course were extremely competitive. Days of interviews, only to be rejected again and again. 'Try again next year. You need more experience. Best of luck next time.' As though they were trying to weed out those who don't really want it. After sometimes years of painstaking application processes, you finally make it on. A minimum three-year course of intense training and work experience. Only to spit you out the other side exhausted, twenty-eight, and still at the bottom.

I swiped my security pass against the door of the hospital I was volunteering at and marched towards the office. Bags and phones were to stay outside in a locker at all times. I felt bright and excited for another day of learning.

I have always been one to take on a lot. Everyone looks at me and thinks, *Are you insane? Running a society, being a course representative, working twenty hours per week as a support worker, and now you want to work for free at a hospital on top of being in your final year at university?*

Yes. I was insane. Completely nuts. Go hard or go home—that was my motto. I wasn't getting a spot on that doctorate course by just completing a degree.

'Hey Linda,' I chirped as I headed towards my little workspace.

'Hiya, Aly. How are you today?' Linda said with a smile that broke through her pained expression.

She was exhausted. Completely and utterly drained. Yet somehow, she found the energy to power through. You see, Linda and I got on very well and one of the reasons why is that we both loved work. We loved what we did. Passion was always high.

After finishing up late again and having to stay in a nearby hotel instead of returning home to her husband, she got about three hours sleep before checking out and driving back to work.

Watching Linda stick her head back into her computer screen again caused an overwhelming sensation to take over my body. Doubt.

Over the coming weeks, I started to closely observe everyone's behavior at the hospital. Other than the patients, who I was observing for completely different reasons, I looked very closely at the staff.

The brilliant nurses who were closing in on their tenth hour. The practitioners who were juggling a million things at once. A battle began to rage within. On one side was the work I was doing in a field I that loved, and on the other was a future I didn't want anymore.

Was I academically ready to face a road to clinical psychology? Sure. I aced my essays every time. I attended every lecture. I was on track for a first class honours degree. But was I ready to sacrifice my early years to get all this?

Doubt soon turned into determination as I realised that my decision to turn my back on my profession and alter in my life's trajectory wasn't really a big deal.

My reasoning went as follows. If I took a year out one of two things could happen:

1. I would find that I really wanted to continue doing psychology and return home to do so.

2. I would discover something more. Something greater than I could ever imagine was possible. Something better? Bigger? Something new that I loved?

This was a no-brainer. The latter wasn't a risk. It was an opportunity. An open door. If the door led to nothing, which was unlikely, then I would backtrack and continue on my previous path. But what if that door led to something incredible? A life that I never thought was possible.

There were people I had never met. Places I had yet to see. Experiences I had yet to have. This new path won. Hands down.

***

Where Is She?

As I sat in my small, cold, damp student digs back in Trefforest, an email popped up from STA travel. Just another marketing email that I normally delete immediately. However, the subject line caught my eye in an instant.

STA travel was giving away twenty-five free working holiday visas with every flight booked to Australia, for one day only. First come, first served.

What was the date? Tomorrow? I checked my savings.

I jumped onto the train to Cardiff at 8am the following day and raced to the STA travel store to be the first in line. An hour later, I had a one-way flight booked out of the country and a free visa to boot.

From that moment on my head was stuck in a journal article or the Lonely Planet's guide to Australia with a highlighter in hand, dreaming of what was to come.

I remember being on holiday in Turkey with my family. Waking up and creeping out of the room to go to the kitchen, my dad would have course be sat on the patio chair, smoking a foreign cigarette and drinking his coffee. A newspaper in his hand would confirm that he had already been out to the shop and picked up some morning supplies. He reminds me a lot of myself now. Always the one to rise up early on holiday, sit outside with a coffee, ready for the day's adventures.

Days that were not spent by the pool involved heading out on a bus or boat to somewhere magical. Stepping out into the blistering heat with my sun hat and factor 50, I would hold my mom or dad's hand and we'd set off somewhere together.

Family holidays became fewer and fewer as my parents' marriage started to break down. I never could imagine their relationship degrading further, but I was proven wrong. Life has a special way of doing that, but I didn't mind so much. Holidays were a privilege, and with so much hostility when we were away, I had one thing I didn't have to dread anymore.

I suppose this all led me to a life of travel. However, even at this point, I had no idea how it all would affect the rest of my early life.

Contrary to popular belief, I do not come from a rich family. The bank of mommy and daddy does not fund my every move across the globe, however much they wish they were in the position to do so. I wouldn't accept handouts even if they were forced on me. I come from a humble two-bedroom rented house in Selly Oak—or Bournville, depending on how you want to look at the street. Either way, I was brought up next door to the Cadbury World chocolate factory and attended a good public school. I had friends. I liked to play in the garden. My parents and I took one holiday a year (if that); many hours and hard work went into making the payments. I am extremely privileged in this sense, to have had the opportunity to get a glimpse at the world from such a young age.

Back when I was eighteen, I had just finished my A-levels and had the whole world in the palm of my hands. Taking a gap year was one of the best decisions I made. It didn't matter that I was working three jobs and travelling was just a dream at the time. I spent eleven months working and saving, and then in my final month before I embarked on the journey to university I decided to go backpacking! First thing's first—I had to book *everything*.

I had four tabs open simultaneously on my aunt's computer. Two were for Easy Jet, and two were for hostels. I had the dates all set out. I had to make sure everything lined up so I had a safe place to sleep every night.

Up until this point, before I went to university, you would not have found any travel websites, YouTube videos or blog posts on first-time travel in my browser history. Sure, I Googled a few things here and there, but what were bloggers? Those people who go to expensive restaurants and then write about how much they hated the duck à l'orange? Blogging wasn't a huge part of everyone's life back then, and even today the suggestion of such a thing still invites the age-old question, 'You're a blogger? What's that?'

I checked. Double checked. Triple checked. OK. Time to book it. I was squirming like an excited toddler. I couldn't believe I was going to do this. My fingers were twitching as I hovered over the 'finalise payment' button. Then a voice entered my head. She spoke harshly towards me, as if I was doing something stupid. I was booking a holiday, not murdering a child.

Aly, have you checked your bank balance recently? You know how much your dad paid for those holidays and how much he would overspend once we were out there! You couldn't afford a two-week trip, never mind a month! What if you run out of money? Do you really want to have to call someone for help? Oh, and FYI, YOU'RE GOING ALONE!

Shut up.

Click.

I held my breath. Did I just book it? I watched the hourglass next to my cursor turn over and then, like a light from heaven, my screen flashed, and I was instructed to print my flight confirmation because I was going to Athens! My heart was racing, and my palms were sweating. But wait, what if my accommodation and return flights sold out while I was there having a tiny congratulations party by myself? Best quickly book it all. So I did. Everything. I was going to Greece!

'Hi Bab, you alright?' My dad's Brummie accent boomed down the phone.

Where Is She?

How do I play this? Subtly? Move in slow; replant the idea of his baby girl travelling around Greece all by herself? Maybe I should give him some time to adjust to the idea? He didn't want me to go to Thailand on my own, but Greece, it's in Europe. Surely he will be fine. Let's be subtle Aly.

'I just booked my ticket to Athens! I leave in twelve weeks!' I screamed.

Slow clap Bravo on the subtlety Aly.

My dad is a large man with an even larger heart. When it came to his little girl, he was delicate, albeit ferociously protective, and you had to tread carefully.

'WHAT? You did *what*?' he said, startled by my greeting.

Shit. Abort, ABORT!

'Yeah, I finally did it. Remember how I said I was looking into Greece? Well, some cheap flights came up, and I just booked it,' I replied as I nervously tried to cover my anxiety.

'Oh. Alright,' he said, still dazed.

Alright? Did he just say, alright? We did it Aly! High five!

'Have you found anyone to go with or is it just you on your own?' he pondered.

Retract high five.

'Just me.' I smiled nervously through the phone.

'Alright then, we'll talk more about it when you come over for dinner. Send me the flight details, OK?'

Mom was the easy one to tell. She has always known deep down that I'm a bit of a free spirit and was expecting the day to come where I flew far and wide.

I was never scared to tell my parents that I wanted to travel. To me, it was just something I could do once I passed my eighteenth birthday. Why wouldn't I want to do it? To experience life beyond the city limits of Birmingham? To me, travel sounded exciting, not scary. A *real* adventure. I would climb mountains and visit ancient ruins that I had only seen on TV. I could try all the local dishes. I wondered what a Greek salad tasted like in Crete and what the sun felt like in Australia.

Little did I know at the time how taking that first trip to Greece at the age of nineteen would affect the rest of my life. Granted, I didn't know how to travel. I pre-booked everything from my flights to the boat transfers. My accommodation was expensive, but it was clean and had a private kitchen. I didn't dare book the cheaper places because they had some bad reviews. I packed way too much and spent far too long in one place. I had no idea what I was doing. Back then, travel bloggers didn't really exist, and YouTube was purely for cat videos. However, that single trip gave me the bug that would absolutely change my life.

Chapter Two

Landing in Melbourne

August 18th, 2013.

I stood in my childhood bedroom looking down at a bag that came up to my thigh, filled with the items I thought would get me through anything that came my way. I did a Shirley Valentine, as I did every time I was about to leave on another adventure. 'Passport, tickets, money, passport, tickets, money.' But this time, it felt different. This time, I had no return flight. I had no itinerary. I had no idea what was in store for me when I stepped off that plane. All I knew for sure was that this was going to be one heck of a ride, and I'd better hold on tight!

-UK to Australia, August 2013

'What on earth are ya doing? Heathrow is miles away! What's wrong with ya?' My dad's Brummie accent repeated the same phrase every summer since I left sixth form. Heathrow airport was miles away from Birmingham, the place I had grown up, but flights were a steal, and I was always OK with taking the long way around to save £50.

Three weeks prior to my departure, I started packing. I did test runs, determined not to forget anything. I had become well adapted to packing for three-week trips through Europe during my summer breaks from university, but I was still a sucker for organising.

Babs, my 70-litre Karrimor backpack stood at my feet, weighing in at 11kg, holding everything I would need for the trip I had been dreaming of for years. I didn't want to leave my room because I could feel my mom's sadness through the bedroom wall. Hauling my backpack onto my shoulders, I made my final trip down the steep staircase, my mom following slowly behind me. The sadness etched on her face broke my heart, but I knew she was proud of me for going after my dreams.

I told my parents that I would be getting to Digbeth coach station by myself. If I couldn't have both of them there without World War Three starting, then it would be easier for me to go alone.

It had been almost five years since my parents separated, and they hadn't seen each other since my graduation. I was anxious enough without having to see them cry as I flew halfway across the world.

My mom never really left the sixties and seventies, and she passed her free-spirited nature onto me, so it came as no surprise to her that I wouldn't be sticking around. My dad, on the other hand, instilled opposing personality traits in me. Punctuality. Get to the airport four to five hours prior to take-off. Always be early.

Daniel would be arriving at Heathrow from Southampton around an hour after me, which was comforting. However, my stomach was still tight with anticipation and anxiety. Daniel and I met a few years back when I was travelling with a girlfriend from university to Italy. We had kept in touch over Facebook and Skype; he was someone who I could truly call a real friend, it didn't matter that Daniel was 10,000 miles away from me at all times. When he heard I would be making my way to Australia around the same time he would be visiting England, we combined forces and booked the same flight out of London to Melbourne.

My heart was racing. This was it. It had finally arrived, August 19th. I was fidgeting in my seat as I stormed down the motorway towards the airport. Then the inevitable niggling thoughts raced through my head.

What if there is something wrong with my visa? What if they don't let me in? Did you forget something? I can guarantee you have forgotten something! Shut up, Aly!

I tried to relax, sink back into the hard seat, and pull out a letter my mom had handed to me before I left, between goodbyes.

'Don't open it till you leave, OK?' she asked.

It read so beautifully; the words of a mother releasing her baby into the big wide world. I knew she would be back at home crying in her bedroom, but I pushed the thought aside, kissed the letter and slid it back into my backpack. Time for the adventure to begin!

I pulled my camera out of my bag as I tried to get comfortable on the cold airport floor and lifted it in front of my face to document the moment. A middle-aged woman pulling her suitcase behind her sat near me. I dropped the camera and blushed. After she left, I tried again, but there were so many people. *Damn it. How do people do this?* I felt like everyone was staring at me. So I gave up and headed to Coffee Club for a pick-me-up.

I sat outside sipping on my milky drink, staring at my £100 camcorder and sighing. I wished that I could film myself in public. So far my YouTube channel consisted of me sitting in my damp uni lodgings, giving people tips from my past trips and teasers for the adventure ahead. I wanted to capture this moment so badly and make videos just like everyone else did on YouTube, but I couldn't. It made me so uncomfortable being stared at that I shoved my camera back in my backpack and accepted defeat.

I headed out to where my coach dropped me, made a nest near a concrete pillar and scrolled through Facebook, waiting for Daniel's coach to arrive. I hadn't seen him in two years; what if I didn't recognise him?

Sure enough, I spotted a man with long, curly hair and silver-rimmed glasses. I lifted myself up to give him a big hug. I had waited to check-in so we could both get a seat together on the flight. Even though it was nice to have a friendly face fly across the globe with me, the knot in my stomach only got tighter.

Three hours into my flight, the attendant placed a rectangular silver tray in front of me, and my stomach quickly made its way to my mouth. I have never been a fussy eater. In fact, people would probably say I overeat. I don't binge, but I certainly enjoy my food. But this silver tray was taunting me. I peeled off the foil only to be greeted with typical airline mush, and I just couldn't stomach it. The smell of Malaysian Delight wafted into my face as I attempted to take a bite. What was wrong with me? This wasn't my first time travelling, so why on earth was anxiety racing through my system? I crumpled the foil back down and lay back into my seat.

***

'Enjoy your stay in Australia!' the bubbly immigration officer said as he handed my passport back to me.

I'm in! I gave myself a mental high five.

By this point, we had been flying for twenty-three hours, and I could barely see straight. I wandered down the wide hall towards the luggage carousels, looking left and right like a lost child. I needed sleep. A tall chap came into my path and asked if I was OK.

'Yeah, I have my declaration card. My friend is getting our bags,' I murmured. *My God, is he going to think I'm drunk? On drugs?!* My eyes were bloodshot, and I had barely taken a bite of food the whole flight.

'Not a problem! Have you declared anything?' he chirped.

I had declared. I declared anything and everything. I had seen *Nothing to Declare* on TV many times. I knew the drill. I wasn't going to prison or be landed with a massive fine. I declared everything right down to the handbag I had, which had a total of four shells sewn onto it.

He glanced at my card and smirked to himself. 'You're fine. Have a great time here!' he said as he passed it back to me.

***

My first morning in Melbourne felt like any other day. I woke up and had absolutely no idea where I was—and then it hit me. *Oh God. What time is it? I need to try to handle any jet lag I encounter. Please don't be late. Please.*

My phone lit up to reveal that it was 9.30am. *Fine. Let's do some stuff then!* I remembered the manager of the hostel handing me a map of Melbourne last night, so I figured out a route to walk into the city and off I went.

Jeans and a T-shirt in the middle of August; I was trying to deny that parts of Australia could actually be cold.

I never like to get on the bus to the centre when I first arrive. I need to ground myself in a place, and the best way to do that is by walking and getting lost multiple times. Plus, I wasn't overly confident about jumping aboard a random tram right away. If I got lost by walking, then I wouldn't have ventured far, but if I jumped on the wrong bus, I could end up miles away. So I started walking.

As I navigated my way around the vast central business district, or CBD for short, I regretted not packing warmer clothes. I had checked Google Weather a million times, but I *still* underestimated how cold 12 degrees could feel.

'Aren't you freezing?' a random voice asked, causing me to spin in every direction to see who was speaking to me.

'Oh no. I'm from England, this is like summer to us!' I laughed through slightly chattering teeth.

The stranger laughed as she made her way across the road, smiling.

OK, so that was stupid. I needed more clothes. I'd add it to the list for tomorrow, and until then, I'd just keep rocking the tinge of blue that appeared on my skin.

Melbourne was fabulous. The tall, glossy skyscrapers contrasted the large murals and epic street art donning every street corner. The smell of coffee wafted from tiny cafes, and the sound of everyday city life raced through the streets.

Finally, back at my hostel, I swung the kitchen door open after a long day of exploration. I was greeted with a few smiling faces. You could tell they were long-term guests by the ease with which they laid around the kitchen and cooked their noodles.

As my legs began to recover from the ache of the day's outing, my conversation in the kitchen was interrupted by the strum of a guitar. I peered outside to see a girl wrapped in a red coat, plucking away. Two thoughts—*I need that coat*, and, *let's join her on the cold ground and admire it close up!*

Little did I know that the girl in the coat was named Allie and that she would soon become a close friend.

Sat amongst my newly made friends, I suddenly felt an overwhelming sense of belonging. Everyone was pitching in together to make dinner. Each of us was talking about our previous adventures and exchanging travel tips over a cheap glass of wine.

We ate 10-cent noodles twice a day, slept on mattresses no thicker than a $10 bill, and sat on dodgy buses for thirty hours—all for the thrill of seeing the world on a $20 a day budget.

Some people enjoy the finer things in life. The five-star hotels with a spa and room service. The comfortable Mercedes taxi rides into the city, where you can pay someone to guide you around the sites, topped off with a three-course dinner surrounded by others at the local tourist restaurant. Who doesn't want that?

But do you appreciate the clean fluffy towels in your hotel room? The peaceful, quiet nights, without roommates who set their alarms at different times and then snooze them repeatedly the next morning before you throw a pillow at them? Do you get excited when you see the free selection of tea and coffee the hotel has provided for your own little kettle? Do you throw your arms up in praise when you realise you have complete freedom to pick from a wide selection of plug sockets located throughout your hotel room, which are yours and yours alone to use?

I do.

Often, when travelling on a budget, you live your life moving from hostel dorm to hostel dorm; sometimes on a daily basis because the hostel you picked can't organise one person to stay in the same room for a week. It's where you try to dry yourself with a micro-fibre towel or sarong that is no bigger than your face, after a shower that took twice as long as it should because you spent the first fifteen minutes playing with the hot and cold taps to achieve a bearable temperature. You're convinced you may die of hypothermia one minute, and feel like you'll have to be rushed to the hospital for second-degree burns the next. Then you try to dress in a space the size of a wardrobe, still dripping, and you drop your jeans on the wet shower floor. You spend the next two hours squeaking about in your wet flip-flops and equally soggy clothes.

Looking around the cramped hostel kitchen, I thought to myself, *Why do we do it?* It's simple really. Because we want to. Because by living below our means, we appreciate the smaller things in life. We adore the little perks, be it a free sample of food at a market or an upgrade from an eight-bed dorm room to a four-share.

However, even though the majority of young travellers live this way on the road, it does not mean they are always happy. Hell, it can get you down at first. Even if you spend your life watching your bank balance and dreading the day the rent is due. When you are in a foreign country, this feeling is amplified. Not only would you have no choice but to go home if you ran out of money, but where would you find the money to *get* home? Or perhaps the scariest feeling is that depleting your savings entirely would mean not only going home, but saying goodbye to travel. Even if it was just for a short while. The moment you start, you honestly cannot stop. Travel grips you at your very core, and she is a harsh mistress. The idea of throwing it all away because of your own stupidity is something that can cripple a traveller.

Once you live below your means, understand it and blossom from it, you can enjoy the greater pleasures in life and truly appreciate them. You don't have to allow money and material possessions to control you, but neither do you have to wear poverty like a medal of honour. After some time, you may realise that having greater pleasures available to you makes you more appreciative of the small ones.

Paying the rent at my hostel, making friends and figuring out the tram system while trying not to run out of money were my main concerns. Honestly, I thought these would be the only challenges.

Oh, how wrong I was.

***

A contrast to Melbourne's dark skies, the Sydney Opera House and Harbour Bridge sparkled under the warm spring sun. Standing in the botanical gardens, I watched as herds of tourists wandered by, taking selfies with Australia's most iconic building behind them. The sun warmed my face, and I basked in the beautiful feeling of contentment that washed over my body.

While I was in Melbourne, an area called Kings Cross was talked about—apparently, it was Sydney's most happening area, and where I needed to be.

Head to the Coca-Cola sign and take a left, I repeated to myself as I wandered the streets, hopefully heading in the right direction.

You couldn't miss it. A bright red billboard all lit up looked like a miniature Times Square as I plodded my way up the hill with my overweight backpack in tow.

Turn left.

As I slowly strolled down the street, keeping an eye out for my new digs, I started to become aware of the fact that something wasn't quite right. Nothing was *wrong* per se, but at first I couldn't put my finger on what was so different. It was just like any other street I had seen, except for the people. The people stood out. I stared down at the pavement, noticing a lady wearing thigh-high boots, paired with a stench of whisky. Then another woman with fishnet stockings up just above her knees.

It soon hit me in my sleepy post-bus daze that I was in the red-light district at 8am, after all, employees had knocked off from a hard night's work.

I giggled to myself as I remembered people recommending this area. *Was it a practical joke?* Regardless, I wasn't too bothered. As I stepped around the ladies of the night and made my way into my hostel, I couldn't stop the grin from spreading across my face.

As a solo traveller, you have to put yourself out there if you want to meet people. So that night, I took to the veranda, which was crammed with benches, tables and old goon boxes.

I got to speak with a couple from France. The conversation wasn't flowing too well—not because of the language barrier. Everyone could speak English pretty fluently, but we just weren't gelling. It happens. They were nice enough. Just no common ground I suppose.

I began chatting with others at the table, and the conversation started to flow somewhat. Then I realised that 90% of the people were from France. It wasn't long till this turned into a problem. It was clear that most of them had been in this hostel together for a while, and eventually, conversation with the British girl faded out. One by one, they turned their backs on me and started talking amongst each other in French.

I attempted to get back into the conversation a few times, but they made it clear that they preferred their mother tongue. I get that. Of course it is more comfortable to speak your native language, but to dismiss someone who you had been *just* speaking to in almost perfect English and turn your back on them—that's just downright rude.

Unfortunately, this was a common theme for the following three nights, which is why I decided to retire early to bed every night for the remainder of my time there.

I was surrounded by so many people, yet I felt so alone. I took this as a lesson. When I would see international students at university either gathering with those of the same nationality or looking extremely isolated while trying hard to be involved, I would understand. As a native English speaker, I have never had an experience a situation where I was defined only by my nationality and language.

A fundamental lesson.

Chapter Three

Scott

Brisbane, Australia. September 2013.

I had slowly been making my way up the east coast of Australia for the past month and had reached Brisbane, where I was soon to start work. I already had a job lined up from a contact back home. Not intentionally, it just happened. During the 2 months between leaving university and arriving in Australia, I worked for a fundraising company, going out onto the streets of Birmingham and getting people to hand over their money. I hated it, but I was really good at it. A guy knew a guy who was now the manager of a fundraising office in Australia. So the job was mine. It didn't last long. It was different in Australia. I just couldn't seem to stop a single person, and I didn't blame them. I never stop.

I had become someone I hated. Hassling people on the street, being pushy and brash was just not a part of my personality. Needless to say, I didn't last the week. It ended with a major breakdown and my boss hugging me in the middle of the city. On the bright side, those stressful days brought some incredible people into my life, people who became life-long friends.

***

I booked into a hostel in Brisbane's trendy West End. Run down? Sure. Cheap? Oh yes. It was by far the most unorganised hostel I had ever stayed at. The reception staff were unable to arrange for one person to sleep in the same bed for just three nights. Every morning I would have to check out and check back in to another room. What a nightmare. Regardless, this was a temporary stay. I had plans to stay a while in Brisbane and start earning some money, so I headed on to Gumtree to find a share house.

Added 2 minutes ago.

What flashed on my screen was no dingy backpacker pad, nor was it miles from the city. I couldn't believe the photographs next to the price. *This can't be real,* I thought. So I messaged the guy as instructed on the ad and went for a viewing the following day.

Searching around for a short while, I came across a high-rise apartment block on the Brisbane River. It had to have been thirty storeys high. I had never been inside one that was so fancy. This couldn't be right. I checked on Google Maps again, and sure enough, it was the correct place.

I phoned the guy, and he came down to let me in. He appeared wearing an XXXX Gold T-shirt, shorts and bare feet. *A stereotypical Aussie,* I thought. We exchanged a few awkward pleasantries in the lift, and he took me to his humble abode. It was a small yet spacious living area with a kitchen that led out to what can only be described as a view of dreams.

Brisbane's Story Bridge was directly in front of me, the water glistening beneath its multi-coloured light display. The apartment was bang in the centre of the city, and so high up you couldn't hear the traffic! I glanced to my left and noticed two beer taps. *No. Surely not.*

Beer on tap and a view to die for. The room was shared, but that was OK for the price.

This was incredible. Landed on my feet? That was an understatement. He handed over the keys, and I agreed to move in the following day!

After my first fundraising job fell through, I went on the look for alternative jobs. Gumtree is a website in Australia that advertises everything from second-hand mattresses to office jobs. It can be a backpacker's best friend or their worst nightmare.

I came across an ad looking for people to do sausage sizzles with the possibility of travelling around Australia. I had no idea at this point what a 'sausage sizzle' was, but it would soon become part of my life for the foreseeable future in Queensland's capital city.

A sausage sizzle is simply a BBQ, normally found outside Bunnings or a supermarket like Coles. They cook up cheap sausages and slap them in a piece of bread with some onions and sauce for around $2.

A cash-in-hand job and a sweet pad to lay my head. I probably celebrated too soon, as my 'dream rental' was about to be smashed just a month after moving in.

I wandered out onto the balcony one morning, took a seat on one of the bar stools and made small talk with Mick. He gave me one-word answers. Actually, for the previous week or so, that's all he had given me.

'Look, Aly, I don't want to go into the reasons behind this, but I don't think this is working out. I think you had better find somewhere else to stay. I don't think it's a good idea for you to stay here anymore. I'll give you back the rent you paid for this week if you leave today,' he said, his face expressionless and emotionless.

My lips parted slightly, but no words came out. Had I just been evicted? What the hell did I do? Utter confusion and anger pulsed through my body. I walked back to my room without another word. I began wracking my brain, trying to think about what I could have possibly done to warrant eviction.

I jumped onto the phone with Mark, a dreadlocked darling whom I worked with during fundraising not long ago. I asked him if there were any free beds at the hostel that he constantly raved about. After asking at reception, the response was a welcomed yes. So I asked him to reserve a bed for me and politely requested his help with moving my things.

After chilling on the rooftop of the hostel, which had now become my home, my phone buzzed. It was Sam.

'Fancy coming for some drinks at the Guilty Rouge?'

Was this a question? Hang out with the old fundraising gang for a few jugs? I was down. This was your standard Wednesday night. No dressing up, just laughs and cold beers.

***

The evening was going well. We were laughing about work and catching up on hostel gossip. Standard things like that. Our conversation was then interrupted by a rather large man and his tall, tanned friend. They asked if they could join us, and of course, we said yes.

They sat down on the opposite end of the long table, and everyone began their introductions. To be honest, I wasn't paying too much attention because I hate conversations on horrendously lengthy tables. So I smiled and tried to join in where I could.

The larger of the two men offered to get us some drinks and came back to the table with multiple jugs. Not once, but several times throughout the night. Large glass beer jugs engulfed the table, and I could tell that things would get messy.

As it reached 10pm, a few of my fellow drinkers departed for bed because they had work the following day. As I stood outside the Guilty Rouge, only my two new friends and I were left.

'What was your name again? Sorry, I am really bad with names!' I asked the tall English lad.

'Scott. What was yours again?' he said, smiling brightly.

'Aly! So, what's the plan? You up for a few more drinks somewhere?'

'Yeah. Sure! Not too sure what his plan is,' he said, pointing towards our larger than life, overly generous friend.

We began to walk towards the high street, Scott and I up front with David on the phone behind us. Scott had only arrived back from his farm work a couple of days earlier, so I suggested we go to The Victory, a classic, cheap and scummy backpacker's bar in the heart of the city.

It was so easy to talk to Scott. I wasn't too sure whether it was the beer or that he was just a chatty guy, but I felt extremely comfortable around him.

After ordering some more drinks, we started talking about travel and our previous movements, until a loud Canadian arrived at our table and started up a random and funny conversation. To this day, I remember very little of what he said to us. Something about work of some sort. What I do remember was that Scott and I suddenly got very close to each other on the sofa-style seat, our shoulders slightly touching while we were laughing at whatever the Canadian guy was saying to us. Scott then leaned over and placed his forearm on my thigh. I stopped breathing for a second. Then I gave him the briefest of looks until I exhaled and looked away.

He didn't remove his arm, and we continued to chat and laugh well into the early hours.

As we walked back towards my hostel, I was telling Scott how great it was to stay there. How good the people were and how it was the perfect place to base yourself. With that, we exchanged numbers and said our goodbyes.

***

I squinted at the all-too-familiar metal-framed bunk bed as I tried to decide whether or not I had a hangover. It was mild. I'd live.

My phone started to buzz while I was sipping a strong instant coffee on the roof; I didn't recognise the number.

'Hello?' I said between slurps.

'Hey, it's Scott,' an English voice came down the phone.

Alyshia Ford

'Who?' I asked, even though I knew who it was.

'Erm, Scott? From last night?' he said quietly.

Why did I ask 'who?' Probably because I cannot function as a human being before my morning coffee and even then it's hit or miss!

We arranged to meet up, and I offered to take him on a mini-tour of Brisbane. I felt some pressure when I elected myself a tour guide. After just over a month, how much did I really know about Brisbane? *More than him, so he won't know any different,* I told myself.

As we strolled over the Queen Victoria Bridge, I remember Scott saying that he had only checked in to Base for a couple of nights. I also remember subtly selling him on Chill.

I don't know why, but I took him to West End even though there is nothing there but bars and restaurants. I thought it would be a good place for him to know about. As we wandered up Vulture Street with the sun in our faces, I saw a Nando's in the distance and I piped up.

'Do you like Nando's?' I asked, presuming he had already visited.

'Never been,' he casually stated

I almost stopped in my tracks. 'Excuse me? Never been to Nando's? Well, I think I'll have to break your peri-peri virginity.' That was my first of many

37

experiences watching Scott battle spice. Even though since then we've adventured through the markets of Indonesia and the backstreets of Thailand, he still can't handle it.

That night there was a party at my hostel where all the backpackers would get thrifty and creative and dress up as werewolves and witches and drink a ridiculous amount of goon. Someone on the roof snapped a good picture of a group of us, so I sent it to Scott. *I wonder what he is doing tonight. Maybe he is lonely. He should come out.*

Signs were posted up around the hostel warning guests not to bring any friends in from outside. I'm not too sure who actually listened to this, but it normally didn't matter; all of your friends were right there anyway. Scott was due to check out of his hostel down the road, so I told him to come and check out Chill. We sat on the roof, and I prayed he wouldn't ask to be introduced to anyone, I *still* couldn't remember half of their names!

We took base in the movie room, and for the life of me, I cannot recall which film was playing. I remember it was dark and the perfect place to sneak our very first kiss. Butterflies fluttered deep in my stomach as Scott wrapped me in his arms, kissing my lips oh so gently. We spent the next twenty minutes cuddled into each other in the dark room, talking, giggling, and smiling.

The saleswoman within me sold Scott on the hostel, so he grabbed his stuff and checked in.

Whenever neither of us was working, we would normally take a walk over to South Bank and either relax on the man-made beach or stroll along the water's edge. Along that side of the Brisbane River, you have the city in all her glory across the water and grass banks with waterside restaurants behind you. We found a particular patch of grass that seemed less popular than the others, and from there it would be known as 'our spot'.

Picnics, stolen kisses and long talks with the most incredible view of Brisbane's skyline in front of us.

A relationship on the road is like no other relationship you can imagine. Intensity is high, as chances are you are staying in the same hostel, which probably means you are sharing a bed.

Shared friends. Shared meals. You are never apart. Now, look at your average relationship back home. You will live apart for maybe years before you take the big step. You will see each other regularly but also have some alone time. That's not how it works when you travel.

With couples that are around each other constantly, you can imagine how many relationships break up after just a couple of weeks. It is a true test. If you can survive living together immediately and are able to give each other the space and time needed to do what you need to do, then you may have something very special.

Scott and I never put any pressure on each other. We were just travelling and having fun. But the inevitable happened, we fell in love.

Love was never part of my plan. I wasn't afraid of my feelings, but I *was* afraid to vocalise them. I never told Scott that I loved him. I was terrified. This was meant to be relaxed and fun. We cared so much for each other, but it was killing me to have these feelings and not tell him. But what if he didn't say it back? What if this was just a short-term fling for him and he ran away screaming? Was I that girl who fell in love only to be rejected?

I called upon the wise and dread-locked guru that was Mark. He knelt down on the roof of Chill next to me as I blurted out my dilemma, Mark smiling massively the whole time.

'Aly, do you honestly not see what everyone else sees?' Mark asked through suppressed laughter.

'What do you mean?' I said, trying not to cry.

'Aly, believe me when I say this. Scott is mad for you. Everyone can see it. Look, we have all seen relationships rise and fall on a daily basis in this hostel. You can tell a mile away that they will never last. But you guys. Urgh, you guys! You guys are *real.*'

'But what if he doesn't say it back?' I asked wide-eyed.

'He will.' And with that, he gave me a kiss on the head and went back to twirling his extinguished fire sticks like the loveable hippy he was.

***

Christmas was just around the corner, and Scott already had his plans set in stone. He was heading to the Gold Coast to spend a few days getting drunk on a massive houseboat, and I was off to Byron Bay with the girls. We decided to have a 'luxurious' Christmas-themed picnic in the park. I told him I wanted to set it up and to meet me at 6pm.

As we were devouring our food and exchanging gifts, I had a knot the size of Birmingham in my stomach. *JUST SAY IT!*

Around twenty minutes had passed, and I just went for it.

'I love you, Scott.'

I held my breath.

'I love you too, Aly,' Scott said, smiling.

Fuck. Breathe Aly. Breathe.

'I just never wanted to put any pressure on us, that's all. But of course I love you!' he continued.

Well, that was easy. What was I worried about? Mark was right. No pressure, but love? Not too sure how that would work. But it did.

Scott and I became long-term guests at the hostel and had the most incredible family of backpackers to live with. Late nights were always followed by everyone sprawling on the wooden benches the next morning, coffee in one hand and exchanging only nods to each other.

It had been around four months since I checked into Chill, and there were times that I thought I was utterly nuts for staying there so long. It was more expensive than a shared house, and I had zero privacy. Scott and I had to share a single bed on the bottom bunk because we couldn't afford a double room. But then I would look around and see the faces of those who had become my family.

Laura, a well-spoken (when she wants to be) British rose. She worked at reception and let us get away with far more than she should have. Her hugs were warm and motherly. We pranced around together with Santa hats one evening and ran screaming naked into the sea at Byron Bay the next, returning only to find that we couldn't locate our clothes. She read beautiful literature and had the warmest of smiles.

Kat, the loudest woman in my life, left her heart wherever she travelled. The epitome of a New Yorker, Kat could tell you a story about a cup and have you splitting your sides with laughter. She was my partner in crime—and in wine. As real as they come, she would hold nothing back. Her smile was infectious, and she loved her hometown so much she should have been paid by the tourism board for a special promotion. Just like there is nowhere like New York, there really is no one like Kat.

Claire reminded me of back home. I don't know what it was about her, but she took me back to where I came from. She was blunt, and I loved that. She was easy to speak to about pretty much anything, and our conversations would roll on through the night.

Tino. He could fight like a Rottweiler and drink like a sailor, but he was one of the sweetest guys in the world. Being a head chef at a fancy restaurant, he first stole our hearts when he would bring boxes of brownies and other sweet treats back to the hostel at 11pm for everyone to enjoy. His Liverpudlian accent was so thick that sometimes you could only smile and nod, wondering what on earth he was talking about.

Jodie, a name well-known in the hostel long before I arrived as she too had been a long-term resident here during her own Brisbane adventures. Along with Laura and Claire, we all went off on a road trip to Byron Bay for Christmas. We all strutted our stuff in Santa hats by day and skinny-dipped under the stars at night.

Looking back, our family was dysfunctional, but it also hilarious, quirky, and loving.

At around the three-month mark, everyone started to move on, break apart and do our own thing. As our little family lost member after member, the hostel began to feel cold and lonely. It just wasn't the same anymore. The joy I experienced while living in Brisbane had absolutely nothing to do with the hostel, but with those who resided within it. Those whom I made memories with. Those who remain friends to this day.

The connections you make while travelling are far more valuable than the sites you see. You could be in a dirty cabin in the woods with no running water, but if you are surrounded by people that you love and cherish, the experience will shift. Likewise, refusing to connect with people you meet will leave you feeling lonely and unfulfilled.

These connections will alter your life without your conscious awareness. The stories you share leave an imprint on those who sit and listen. A ripple effect silently occurs throughout your lifetime—a story, a friendship, a confrontation, they all leave their footprints life, slightly or violently shifting your feet from y are currently walking without you even

An expensive apartment with one of the best views in Brisbane will mean nothing if you are not sharing it with people you feel connected to. I moved from that apartment into a budget hostel and shared a room with seven other travellers for four months. It won hands down as some of the best months I have had while travelling.

The simple fact is that those around you will make you associate certain emotions with any given place. The more friendships you form and people you connect with, the more vivid those memories will be.

The greatest stories—the ones that you will cherish and laugh about later—generally do not include entry into a national park or getting the perfect shot of yourself with The Leaning Tower of Pisa. They will be the late nights in the hostel playing cards with your new friends on the roof while learning how to swear in several different languages. They will be the group of Irish backpackers you met at the airport and ended up hanging out with when you arrived at your new destination.

When I look back on my time in Brisbane now, my mind floods with memories from Chill, the weird and wonderful characters I met, and the strange family we became. Not the attractions or museums. *The people.*

Chapter Four

Blackall

Blackall, Australia. January 2014.

*I have everything a working holidaymaker could ask for—
an hourly paid job in the heart of a bustling city, an amazing
group of friends and the man of my dreams waiting at home
for me every day. So I decide to pack up and leave everything
to work an almost identical job in the middle of nowhere.
Seventeen hours inland from the coast of Queensland in an
Outback town called Blackall.*

*I have to take this path on my journey. I have to move off
the beaten track. After five months, I have to see Australia.*

Slumped over my £90 Dell Netbook that struggled
to boot up every day, I realised that I was wasting my
time. I scrolled through the endless advertisements on
Gumtree: 70% were scams, 10% were jobs nobody
would ever want, and 10% were unpaid, which left
backpackers with only a handful to apply for.

BACKPACKERS, WE NEED YOU!

Nope.

**WANT TO EARN MONEY AND TRAVEL
AROUND AUSTRALIA?!**

Yes, but no.

DO YOU LIKE MEETING NEW PEOPLE AND DRINKING BEER?

OK, I *did* click on this one. Still no.

TOPLESS BARMAID REQUIRED $50 PER HOUR.

Hmm. I mean, no.

It didn't take me long to narrow my search down to four potential jobs. I emailed them all my standard response, attached my CV and waited. It didn't take long for the first position, located all the way up in Cape York, to message me back. Some guy wanted a cleaner and cook (basically a wife) in exchange for $50 per day with bed and board. Cape York, situated at the very tip of Australia, can only be accessed by four-wheel drive. Dark thoughts of being trapped in the middle of nowhere with a random single man and no way to get out crossed my mind. Surprisingly, it was quite a struggle to turn down that job. I like weird and wonderfully deserted areas to explore.

It wasn't until the next day that my next destination would be set in stone when a young girl named Cassey called me.

'Hello?' I enquired excitedly, as an unknown number surely meant a job offer.

'Hiya! Is this Alyshia?' a thick and bubbly Queensland accent boomed down the line.

'Speaking,' I said

'Hiya Alyshia, you applied for a job as a barmaid yesterday in Blackall?'

'Yes. Yes, I remember!' The application stood out because they asked me to send a photo along with my CV. I'd never been asked to include one before.

'Great. This is Cassey. My dad runs the pub, but he asked me to give you a ring because he's down in Brisbane at the moment,' she chattered.

After a twenty-minute chat with Cassey, we both seemed happy to accept the position, but first, she had to check with her dad when he got back. Whenever this happens, you either won't hear back, or they call you three weeks later, horrified to learn that you accepted another job. My call was returned the next morning, and it was settled. I was going to Blackall.

Where the hell is Blackall? I asked myself.

After looking at Google Maps, I found out that it was smack bang in the middle of Queensland. Was I about to venture into the real Australian Outback for the first time? I Googled 'Outback' to see which towns met the criteria. Wikipedia was not too helpful. It merely provided a description of the Outback—dry, red, dusty, etc. I would look out for these indicators when I arrived. If Blackall was indeed dry and red, I could make it Facebook official, but not a minute sooner.

Blackall was a simple, small country town famous for its wool export back in the day. For me, it would be a place where I would meet both despicable characters and shining stars. Laughter, racism, new friends, sexism and homophobia would make this western gipsy run screaming in the other direction just two months after arriving.

One thought weighed heavily on my mind—my method of transportation into Blackall. It turned out that the owner, Chris, made weekly trips into Brisbane to pick up alcohol—apparently much cheaper than getting it delivered to the middle of nowhere. We delayed my start date and agreed that Chris would pick me up the next time he was swinging through the city. This felt very odd. Never before had I placed my faith in complete strangers who (may or may not have) lived in the Outback.

Cassey's parting words concerned me even further. 'When I go with my dad we normally camp out overnight and sleep somewhere. I'll throw my swag in the truck for you to sleep in!'

After another Google search for the term 'swag', which I discovered to be an open sleeping bag type affair, my worry started to grow. *Who are these people? Why did they want my picture? I don't know them, and one will be picking me up in a truck, driving me seventeen hours away and stopping off en route to sleep on the streets?*

Where Is She?

A tug of war raged deep within, between my gut screaming for an adventure and my intuition planting question marks on my every decision.

***

I stood waiting at the pre-arranged train station. It was an uncharacteristically cold day for Brisbane, and my backpack started to soak up the morning dew on the ground. I looked up and down the long residential street, my stomach in knots over the impending arrival of my new boss. I wasn't dramatic enough to think that he would be an axe-wielding murderer. I fear far less important matters. *What if he doesn't show? It's been ten minutes now. Seventeen hours in a truck with a stranger.* My confidence in my people skills was fading rapidly. I can hold a conversation, but for seventeen hours?

The large whooshing sound of a truck's engine and breaks interrupted my irrational yet terrifying thoughts. At that moment, the sound bought some comfort and took me back to childhood trips I took in my dad's truck. I pulled my head back, peering into the cabin so I could finally put a face to the name.

He didn't look like a murderer. But then again, I suppose they never do.

A short man with thin black hair and a face etched with worry lines greeted me with an endearing crooked smile. I pulled myself up into the cabin, backpack hoisted on one shoulder, threatening to unbalance me at any moment.

'I'm sticking you on tomorrow tonight. It'll be good for ya. Throw you in the deep end! Should be a good crowd!' Chris informed me.

What day was it? Friday. I swallowed hard. It doesn't matter how many bars you work in, you still have to get used to how things flow in each place, and this place would be like no other I had ever worked in.

'On Fridays, you can wear what you want, within reason!' said Chris.

Oh great, I thought. *What do I have? What's not too short but gives a 'Friday night' feeling?*

Nothing. I had absolutely nothing.

'We'll be pulling up soon. Bet you can't wait to get out and stretch your legs, eh?'

'It'll be good!' I smiled back.

I liked Chris. We'd only known each other for around twelve hours, but I could tell he was genuine. He was the kind of guy that was not fazed by much, or at least he wouldn't show it. He laughed a lot. Whether it was because he was genuinely content with life or if his laughter stemmed from nervousness, I wasn't sure.

'I think Cassey put her swag in here for ya,' Chris mumbled as he searched the back of the cab.

My feet hit the dusty ground, and as I raised my eyes, my heart stopped. An explosion of diamond-like stars dotted the inky night sky for as far as the eye could see.

Chris rolled out what seemed to be a very thick sleeping bag, sturdy in its structure yet very open to the elements.

'I'm just going to the toilet,' I said as I trotted off to the small public loos.

Cautiously, I stepped around the large puddles and pushed the door open with my fingertip, only to be greeted by two very adorable little green frogs perched on the toilet seat. I took a step towards the porcelain throne, thinking they would move immediately. I was wrong. I tried to nudge them off with my finger gently, but they barely moved an inch. That night I shared a toilet seat with two frogs.

Skipping back to where Chris had set up our sleeping area, I nestled into Cassey's swag. It was surprisingly comfortable, I lay there watching the stars and slowly drifted to sleep.

What felt like a split second later, I heard a loud thump next to my head that disturbed my hazy nap. My eyes slowly shot to my right as I heard two more thumps, this time further away. Peering through the dark, allowing the street lamps to light my view, I saw the outline of a kangaroo only a metre from my swag. *Are you kidding me?* My heart raced with pure excitement as the 'roo hopped off into the darkness.

'What are the chances a kangaroo would pass right next to my head?' I asked Chris while rubbing my eyes in the morning sun.

'Ah, you saw one did ya? Most likely. Everywhere they are!' he chirped.

This is going to be great.

***

When we arrived, I found, to my utter shock, that the reason they requested my photo was to see whether I fitted their criteria. I was deemed slim and attractive, and apparently, boys in that town only came to the pub to drool at the foreign meat. An 'ugly' girl wouldn't attract the punter, and a 'fat' girl could never stand on her feet all day, or so I was told.

'I showed all the boys your photo,' Cassey said over her shoulder, grinning a wild, teasing smile.

Oh God. Why? What boys?

Too many questions ran through my mind in a single instant. I pushed them aside and put on my game face.

Where Is She?

Feeling like a third wheel, I ploughed through the night, serving multiple shots and trying to suss out the crowd. They were loud, but it was a Friday after all, and they seemed to enjoy the light-hearted banter, which was always fine with me. Retiring to bed after helping clear down the bar, I had survived my first shift. My aching legs welcomed the soft bed sheets as I the silence of the night lulled me into a deep sleep.

***

'Right, I'll show you how to open up tomorrow. For today, let's get these fridges stocked up! It's something you can do whenever—just so you have something to do!' Cassey informed me.

'OK, so just write a little list and go into the cold-' Cassey continued before I politely interrupted.

'No problem, I have worked in a few pubs. I'll get this done!' I said proudly.

'Go for gold, mate! You'll do alright here!' she said as she made her way around to the other side of the bar and sat on a stool.

I like Cassey.

Lemonade...where is it? Great. Just when I tell Cassey how well versed I am in bartending, and I can't even find the cans of lemonade.

I remembered instantly what Cassey had told me before we started the shift.

'Have you ever worked in a country pub before, Aly?' she enquired.

'No. Only small pubs and one big city pub,' I said bashfully, thinking I had done something wrong.

'Right! Well, OK. There are a few big things you need to know,' she said as she strode into the bar area.

Cassey educated me on country pub ways. The three rules she espoused would soon be the commandments I would have to follow while working there.

'Firstly,' she said 'be prompt. Actually. Be extra prompt. Regulars do not like waiting for a drink. As soon as they place that glass on the bar, you better be getting their next one ready.'

But how do I know if they want another one? I wondered, but stayed silent.

'Second', Cassey continued, 'if their glass is upright with money next to it, they want another. Hand over a fresh drink and take the money, no need to ask. And finally, if their glass is laid down on its side, they are done. No more drinks.'

'ALY!?' a voice yelled. I was about to meet my first regular.

I poked my head through the window in the cold-room to see Cassey pointing to a very small, bearded man with a cap on.

'This is Dave,' Cassey said, smiling from across the bar.

'Hi! My name's Aly!' I exclaimed in my cheeriest of voices.

'Nice to meet you darl'. Usual please.'

'Alright,' I said bashfully looking over to Cassey who had already come to my side.

'Dave has his drinks in one of these,' Cassey said, as she reached into the cabinet and pulled out a very small glass.

'OK...'

'No one else really has these glasses. That's why there is only a few of them,' Cassey explained.

Right, OK. So these little 8oz glasses are for Little Dave. I can remember that. I came to pour from the taps that were positioned on the back wall behind the bar. At first, I hated that I had to turn my back to the customers while serving, but I would soon learn to love this aspect because I could freely pull faces at some of the patrons behind me.

Dave was a lovely soul. A tiny gentleman with tiny glass, but he was genuine. He provided me with plenty of heartfelt conversations over the following nine weeks. This was going to be good.

I ran through my daily to-do list in my head. *Take tills out of safe. Switch tills on. Unlock bottle shop door. Take specials board and place near road. Stomp across the 'dance floor'. Switch on the jukebox. Unlock back door. Turn on lights in toilets. Take stools off bar. Place bar mats neatly across bar top. Unlock front door. Unlock side door. Put four bar stools out in smoking area. Write daily lunch special on chalkboard.*

***

The heavens decided to open in Blackall for the following three days. It would finally give people something to talk about. Something other than how hot it was, how business was shit or how this silly Pommy (Aussie slang for a Brit) wouldn't be able to handle the heat.

As I slowly paced around the island in the middle of the bar, my ears pricked up to the sound of the front door swinging open. I spun around to see three unfamiliar faces enter. All three men wore black and were talking to each other as they walked towards the bar, taking their final position on the right-hand side where I greeted them as I do everyone.

'Y'alright love? What can I get ya?'

'Three pots of Gold,' he demanded, staring deep into my soul.

'No problem!' I said, forcing a cheerful demeanour.

Pulling out three pot glasses at once, I started to slowly fill them, listening over my shoulder to the strangers rambling.

'I ain't complaining! But fuck, money ain't going to be too good, eh!' the middle one exclaimed while gesturing towards the heavy downpour of rain outside.

Upon returning to them with their requested drinks, I noticed a $20 bill waiting for me on the bar. As I reached out my hand to collect the note, they all stopped talking and stared at me. I tried to ignore the stares and proceeded to get their change.

I gave them the benefit of the doubt. I peered at the clock. *Five hours to go. Come on.* I started to wipe down the island and the bar when I heard a wolf whistle from behind me. The three men were vying for my attention.

Oh hell no. You did not just whistle at me!

At the same moment, another customer placed his empty glass on the bar in front of me, which I picked up and took to the back to re-fill. A whistle pierced my ears again. I ignored them. *How dare they? Do not even think that any of you will get my attention by whistling at me.*

I could hear their mutters turning from senseless drivel to irritation and astonishment at my apparent deafness.

'Oi!' the middle guy shouted.

My blood pressure shot through the roof, and I'm sure my face started to turn crimson. My hands began to shake as adrenaline raced through my veins. I knew what was coming. I knew what I had to do. They wouldn't like it, but it would give me a lot of satisfaction.

I continued to ignore them as I aimlessly wiped down random surfaces behind the bar, trying to control my trembling extremities.

'Excuuuuuuse me?' the middle one piped up again.

I spun quickly on my heels and headed towards the three men.

'Yes, darling what can I get you?' I said, putting on the fakest smile I could muster.

The middle guy and his two cronies pulled back slightly from the bar and looked at each other, smirks spread across their faces as if to say, 'What the hell? Why do you think we've been whistling at you, bitch?'

'I'm neither a dog nor a taxi, so I don't respond to whistling. Now, same again?' I snapped before they had the chance to reply. I didn't even crack a smile.

The three faces dropped to the floor. I grabbed their glasses and refilled them with XXXX Gold before they could collect their thoughts and respond.

When I got back, their facial expressions had changed from utter shock to disgust. I'm sure a young, out-of-town woman, had never had the audacity to speak to them in such a manner. They looked at me as if I was dirt. How dare a *woman* actually speak back to a *man* in such a way? How dare a woman have standards, a voice, and power over them?

I walked out to the dining room for a second to slow my nerves and to silently congratulate myself on my quick wit. I was only away for minutes. When I returned, the men were gone. Only three empty pot glasses remained.

No tip.

***

It was another quiet day, and I thought, *Screw it, there's less than a handful of people in the bar, there's no sport on, so I'm going to have a flick through! ELLEN! Yes. She has another A-lister on. I don't follow celebrities much. I'm guessing he is in a new blockbuster coming out soon.*

'Urgh! Turn that fucking dyke off, NOW!' a man shouted, spitting through his words.

'Excuse me?' I exclaimed.

I can't hold my tongue where bigotry and homophobia are concerned. I can't. I respected Chris, and these were regulars, but I didn't give a shit. Homophobes gave me the fucking chills. I wanted to put their heads in large blenders.

'That woman. Liking other women, fucking disgusting. Turn it off!' he continued.

I put the remote control down and turned to him.

'No.' I said.

He opened his mouth slightly

'It's not my problem that you aren't educated enough to see that there is nothing wrong with homosexuals. I love Ellen. I don't see her as a lesbian. She is just Ellen, a human being. She gives lots of free stuff to people. I like her. Get over it.'

He grumbled for a while.

'It ain't natural, urgh. Just pick anything else will ya?' he barked.

'Look, there isn't any sport on, so I will lower the sound just in case her gay voice upsets you, OK?' I said in the most sarcastic tone I could muster.

There wasn't much more mentioned on the topic, except for a few grumbles here and there.

I need to get out of here, I told myself.

I see now that working in Blackall quickly turned from an Outback adventure to nothing more than a paycheck. I struggled to connect with anyone apart from a handful of locals. It was a different world, one where I felt like I didn't belong. I was doing it for the money. Absolutely nothing else was keeping me there.

A job expels a lot of your energy and even more of your time. It can get to a point where a paycheck is not enough of a reward for what the job can take from you. If your job is sucking the life out of you every time you clock on, if you get very little in return for a job that requires you to sacrifice your life, then you are headed for a downward spiral.

Looking back, I wish I could have found a way to enjoy it more. Hindsight is a fine thing. Granted there was little opportunity for fun when I was working sixty-plus hours a week and could count the friends I'd made on one hand, but it was simply a means to an end. A way for me to keep travelling. Don't get me wrong, I learnt a lot from my time there. I listened to others' opinions, whether I agreed with them or not. I got an opportunity to talk to a lot of people doing what I did, but it was never enough. The small town of Blackall just wasn't a place I could thrive, no matter how many locals I chatted with or how many lessons I tried to learn from my time there.

That's when it hit me. Looking around the bar, I saw my story in too many people. The only difference was that they had no end goal. Just another paycheck. Another day, another dollar. All I could think of is that I could not live my life that way.

At this point, I was still unaware of how exactly I would create a life where I did what I loved, but the idea of crafting a life where I wasn't ruled by the nine to five grind was high on my to-do list. I felt that through travelling, my mind would begin to open up to opportunities that I had never considered before. The more jobs I took, the more I learnt about myself. The idea of running home to pick up where I left off in terms of my education was fading.

Where is this path taking me? I pondered while cleaning down the bar one quiet Tuesday night. Then like a rock, it hit me hard in the chest. My path is not predetermined. For me, there is no grand plan. No outer force pushing me towards my end goal. That force was within me. I had to pave my own path in life. Brick by brick, I would have to be the one to start building a path that led me to where I wanted to be.

Every step I took and every brick I laid meant I could have whatever I wanted. I could decide on the destination, and I could pave the journey. The only question that remained was where. My next step would shed more light on my path.

Chapter Five

Layna and I

Ilfracome, Australia. April 2014.

After two months of living the rural roller coaster that was Blackall, a small, nagging voice still lingered in the back of my mind. *Eighty-eight days of farm work.*

Travellers who are looking to extend their working holiday visa must complete eighty-eight days of rural work to qualify. There had been no opportunities in Blackall, and I was adamant that I wouldn't be doing fruit picking for $1 per bucket. As I scrolled through listing after listing online, I finally smacked my head against my laptop.

Scams. Volunteer positions.

I knew one thing; I was going to be paid for whatever job I took. I was no stranger to hard work and working on a station or bending over picking strawberries required you to work long hours in horrendous temperatures.

Long days behind the bar were dragging me down, so I used something that had been listed as one of my skills on my resume for years: initiative. *Screw scrolling for hours on Gumtree. I'll put up my own ad.* Within twenty-four hours, I had four job offers to choose from. Which one was paying a decent wage? What type of job was I willing to do? I phoned a woman who emailed me her number if I wished to discuss a position on her organic farm.

'Hello?' a high-pitched voice echoed through the end of the phone.

'Hi there, my name is Alyshia. You responded to an ad I placed on Gumtree? I am an English backpacker looking to complete my eighty-eight days of farm work.'

'Oh, yes. Hi. OK, so the position will be mainly in the house with me. I own my own business, and I am extremely busy,' she rattled.

'Right, OK...'

'So there will be a little bit of work in the garden, but for the rest of the time I will need an assistant to help me run my business from home.'

Great. I can do this. Own business, eh? Nice wage, little work inside, little work outside.

'That sounds great. I have office experience, and I would be happy to help. What would the living arrangements be like and what's the pay?' I sheepishly asked.

'Right, well, we will give you your own room and your meals in exchange for the work you do.'

Hold up; excuse me? You want me to be your assistant, work on your tiny organic farm and tend to your garden, all with only room and board in return? My head jolted back, but I remained silent. This was laughable. If I wasn't raised to be so polite, I would have slammed the phone down.

'Right, OK. That will be a problem. I have expenses of my own, and for the hours I put in and the amount of future travelling I have planned, I am looking for *paid* work at this time,' I said blatantly, as though I was explaining some foreign concept that people are generally paid to work full-time.

'Well, it's not paid. Sorry about that,' she replied

'OK, thanks for your time,' I said wistfully as I ended the call.

Sure, a lot of other backpackers work for accommodation, but I am not every other backpacker. I *know* my worth, and I *know* my rights. If I am to slave away in the heat, being cut up, bruised, burnt and exhausted, I want to be compensated with that rare and wonderful paper stuff we cram into our wallets. I was not free labour, and I started to get sick to death of all these employers who just wanted to take travellers for a ride. They know how much we want our second-year visa, so they think they can scam us.

Left doing your three months till the last minute? You are prime bait to them because you are desperate. Plan ahead.

Right, next.

'Ello?' a deep Aussie accent drifted through the phone.

'Hi, could I speak to Lenor please?' I beamed.

'She's not here right now. She went into town,' he replied.

'OK, erm, my name is Alyshia. I posted an ad on Gumtree as I am looking to complete my rural work, and I got an email from Lenor?'

'Ah right, I see. Good. OK, well if I can take your number, I'll get her to call you back sometime this evening. Might be tomorrow. Depends on what time she gets back.'

'That's great, thank you.'

After giving him my number, I held out some hope. I prayed she wouldn't call back while I was on my shift, which was to resume in fifteen minutes. It's hard to explain, but sometimes when you're travelling, you just fancy a break. A holiday of sorts. It sounds ridiculous, but remember, I was working fifty hours per week in a town that was becoming less and less attractive.

I relieved the other barmaid, and not a minute too soon as we had a grand total of *two people* in the bar. There is nothing worse than working a ten-hour shift and serving approximately ten people.

My mind drifted. My thoughts turned to all the places I would like to go. The sound of the sea adding one of nature's beautiful soundtracks to the evening. Live music on stage; the strumming of an old guitar. A large glass of Shiraz in an oversized tulip glass, slightly burning but exciting my tongue as I raise its thin stem. The warm breeze tingling as it caresses my cheeks.

My state of utter imaginary bliss was interrupted by a *tap tap tap* sound.

'Oi, love!' grunted one of the regulars as he banged his glass on the bar.

If there is one thing that annoys me most about working behind a bar, it's rude people.

'Fucking hell. Not like you've got anything else to do 'round 'ere! Only two of us and you can't even pay attention,' he slurred in a semi-playful manner.

'I was in a better place! Now calm down, you had barely taken your last swig before you started banging it around,' I exclaimed in a not-so-playful manner.

He smirked as I took his change from the bar. *God, I need to get out of here. Fuck it, I'm going to Melbourne.*

Within twenty-four hours, I had booked my flight and arranged to stay with Daniel.

I slumped off after my shift to my tiny room upstairs and looked through my missed notifications on my phone.

New Voicemail Message.

Damn it.

'Hi, Alyshia? It's Lenor here. How ya doing? Just giving you a ring back. If you want to give me a call tomorrow, I should be in all day. Thanks.'

After a rather pleasant conversation, I agreed to start work for her and her husband in two weeks' time. It worked out well for both of us as I wanted to go back to Melbourne for a mini break and she had some loose ends to tie up before they needed me.

'What kind of property is it?' I asked.

'We are a sheep station. Got about five-thousand sheep, and with my son being away travelling, we could both do with a hand. So you will do some jobs for me, but a lot of the time you will be out with Peter. We have two rounds of shearing coming up, so we need an extra pair of hands. We pay $400, and your bed and board are included.'

I could finally breathe.

Where Is She?

***

The dust swirling around the bus was a comforting sight, which had been slightly tainted by recent experiences. The stark contrast of city life in Victoria's capital and the dessert planes that stretched for as far as the eye could see comforted me. I love big cities. The excitement, the rush of the crowd. But it gets old real quick. I was a traveller. I could move when I felt like it, and I enjoyed the harsh Outback landscape one week and a cold beer in hand overlooking the Yarra the next.

Melbourne was the perfect break even though my new job was literally an hour or so down the road from Blackall and making a trip to a different state seemed slightly counterproductive. I got to see civilisation again and catch up with Daniel over long chats and hot coffees. Melbourne became my favourite city, a place where I could spend days wandering around quaint suburbs, watching the locals go about their daily business with a flat white in hand.

***

Peter arranged to meet me at the bus stop in Longreach. He was a tall, stocky man with a smile as white as his hair. He seemed to have a limp but showed no outward sign of pain in his movement towards me. No matter how seasoned you are as a traveller, driving into the middle of nowhere and being picked up by a totally random stranger will always put an ill feeling in the depths of your stomach. This feeling subsided when I arrived.

Lenor was running a couple of errands, but after dropping my backpack at the ute, we arranged to all meet at the Marino Bakery for a coffee.

As I wandered through my new surroundings, I tried to picture what Lenor would look like. A stockman's wife. Shorts and a long-sleeved shirt, perhaps? Her clothes would show the wear and tear of Outback life. No make-up. Hair tied up in a bun.

I was brought back out of my daydream when Peter's arm flew up to call over a short, dark-haired woman dressed in deep blue jeans and a crisp shirt. Her hair was short and close to her head and was well maintained. The make-up she wore was subtle yet bold. Her heeled boots clicked and clacked towards us, and she gave me a warm, motherly smile.

'Have we ordered?' Lenor asked Peter.

'Yes, three coffees and a couple of cakes are on their way,' Peter replied.

Lenor turned to me. 'Have you ordered food? Are you hungry? It must have been a really long coach ride, so order what you want, really!' she beamed.

'Oh, it's OK, I ate on the bus. I could just really do with a coffee right now. Thank you so much though,' I politely declined.

Unfortunately, Lenor had to shoot off to the airport and fly to Brisbane, but she left me some odd jobs to do around the place until she got back.

Peter and I finished our coffees before heading to the farm.

Not much surprised me. I had become quite accustomed to the Outback. Peter showed me the bedroom I would call home for the next three months. A medium-sized room with double doors, double bed, AC and a little en-suite. Lovely. I stuck my head into the little bathroom area and noticed a little green frog balancing on the shower rail.

'Oh, hello there!' I said to the little critter.

He wasn't the chatty type.

'Sorry mate,' I continued out loud, 'but I need a shower. You are more than welcome to join me, but you will have to shimmy over,' I said as I slowly pulled the shower curtain. Fredrick leapt out of the way and found a nice corner to sit and wait for me to finish. From then on, all frogs were called Fred.

That night I lay on my bed and breathed a sigh of relief. *This is great. Nice people. Nice house. This has worked out perfectly.* My musings were interrupted by a foreign sound coming from outside my door. I peered out and walked towards the back steps. *Frogs? Big frogs?* A deep, rumbling croak came from multiple directions. As my eyes adjusted to the night sky, large wart-covered toads came into focus. Not just one, but many. Strewn across the gravel path, a chorus of cane toads sang me their song. I sat perched on the top step, looking at the night sky while these strange, *ugly* creatures serenaded me.

***

As a seasoned traveller, you'd think my sense of direction would be above par. Trotting around different cities and tiny towns all the time, I should have this down to a tee. All of those who have been in a car with me, walked next to me through a city or have seen me cross a street will know that sometimes I can be like a bird flying West for winter. Thankfully, I can now appreciate the art of getting lost in a foreign country. Mainly because I have no choice in the matter.

In Ilfracombe, people used the sun to get a perspective of direction, but I was always told to never look at it directly. I was unable to 'read the sun', and there were no proper roads to speak of, nevermind road *signs*.

My first solo job on the property was to head off in the ute, grab some logs and wire along the way and patch up the kangaroo holes along one of the fence lines. It was a scorching-hot day, and I was in my own little bubble. I was driving 10ft, stopping, grabbing my log and wire, and whistling the sounds of some made up tune from deep in my brain.

Two hours later, I ran out of wire, so it was time to head back for smoko. Smoko, as the Aussies call it, is a mini break between the time you start and lunch. The Aussies know what they're doing. Coffee, fruit bun, and then back to work.

Upon re-entering the vehicle, I noticed a U-turn or ten-point turn wouldn't be possible, and I also noticed that the road looped around up at the top. So in my mind, I thought, *Well obviously that will loop back to this road at some point, and I'll be homeward bound.*

I drove and drove, slowly realising that I was *slightly* lost. Then I came upon a tank that I had never seen before and lost sight of the fence I had been patching. I quickly realised that I was *really fucking lost*.

I thought to myself, *if I stop, then I'll be seen as having no idea what I'm doing with my life.* So I just kept driving. In the middle of nowhere. Just red sand and lots of trees.

Then, like some glint of heaven, I saw a flash of green. It could only mean one thing—Peter had come to rescue me! I was happy to see him zooming towards me. It was then I noticed that he was smiling manically. I think I turned a unique shade of rouge.

'Taking the scenic route eh?'

He had seen me pass the tank only five minutes previously, going on my own little adventure. It reminded me that someone, somewhere is always laughing at you, so you better make sure you are laughing too!

***

'Have you seen a kangaroo yet?' Peter asked.

I always hated when people asked me that. I never knew how to respond. The excitement in their eyes, being the first one to introduce a Pom to their country's national animal. Yes, I had seen a lot. I had fed them from my hand back in Blackall and had seen them leap in front of road trains like the suicidal cuties they are.

'A few back in Blackall, yeah!'

'Well, you are in for a surprise. We have a few more here than Blackall does.'

He wasn't wrong. Over the coming months, I would witness thousands of 'roos, dodge them with my truck, watch them bounce beside the ute at 50km per hour, and patch up the never-ending holes they would create in the fence.

They were everywhere. They easily outnumbered the stock by two to one, if not more. No wonder there was a drought; 'roos dominated the water holes all day, every day.

Where Is She?

I did my best to avoid hitting them when I was driving around the property, but my luck ran out when I had to put one out of its misery with a single shot of led.

'Oh my God,' I cried as Peter and I pulled up to a dried-up dam in the middle of the property. Completely empty of water, the torso of a grey 'roo stuck out of the mud with its legs stuck deep down below him.

'Urgh. He probably wandered into the middle of the dam to reach the last drops of water and got bogged.'

The mud was rock hard around his waist. Poor thing had easily been there for a couple of days. In front of him were scratches indicating that he had tried to free himself. Under the harsh heat of the Outback, he was on death's door, and my heart couldn't take it anymore.

Peter headed towards the ute to retrieve his rifle. 'Do you want to do it?'

I looked back over my shoulder to the saddest sight I have ever seen in my life. I debated quickly in my head whether I could take his life. He was suffering more than any animal should.

'Yep,' I said quietly.

Peter made me do some practice shots before letting me point the gun at the dying 'roo.

One squeeze and he fell asleep.

***

The first sheer of the year was fast approaching, and the whole family was preparing for what would be a very tough time, both physically and mentally. The week would involve drenching the dirt in the paddock next to the sheds where the sheep would be held. Then we had to muster the first lot of sheep from their paddocks to the shearing sheds. We would pick up some random sheep along the way, so we would need to draft them into groups so that any stranger stock could be collected by their rightful owners on nearby properties. Once the first batch was ready to go, the shearing team would arrive early and start their work. As soon as the sheep came down the chute, we would take the small herd and push them into the run to be drenched (a process to kill worms). After drenching, it was time for the sheep to run free as we mustered them back to their paddock.

However, before the work was to commence, Peter had to check the location of his stock. He obviously had a good idea of what paddocks they were in, but he needed specifics and to see if any strays were wandering about of their own accord. The best way to do so was from the sky. The plane that slept in its hanger for months would finally be fired up.

Peter told me that I wouldn't be able to go up with him when shearing started. He needed to fly close to the ground, and it wasn't viable or entirely safe. However, he did have to take the plane for a spin before he took it out for mustering.

Yes!

After some maintenance and safety checks, I jumped in and had my phone gripped tightly to film the epic flight!

Up until this point, I had been gathering footage where I could in hopes of creating some epic videos for my channel. The only problem was that in such a rural area the internet was capped at a very low download limit, which meant my hopes of uploading my adventures was slim to none. Regardless, I found such excitement in capturing my experiences even if it did mean waiting another two months to upload them.

The ground disappeared beneath the aircraft, and the red dust travelled further and further away. We were flying! I was in my own bubble looking around, seeing the great plains of the Queensland Outback stretched out all around us. Not a hill nor a green patch in sight! Peter then broke my train of thought.

'Want to have a go?' he shouted over the noisy engine.

I froze. *Have a go at what?* I looked around us. *This? This plane? You want me to...what?*

'OK!' I said before I knew what I had agreed to.

'You just have to keep it straight!' Peter explained as he pointed to a dial.

I grasped the control wheel and out of the corner of my eye, I saw Peter letting go of his. *I'm doing it. I'm flying a plane!*

Adrenaline rushed through me as I clenched my jaw tight in the hope that it would make me focus. A few corrections from Peter were needed, but this flying thing was pretty easy.

Too easy? Oh Lord, I'm going to crash. I clenched my jaw tighter.

We eventually got back to the house where Peter took control again and landed like a pro.

The adrenaline continued to pulse, and I couldn't stop shaking. No words could describe how incredible I felt at that moment. I just couldn't wait to see what else this place had in store for me.

***

My eyes opened slightly as light filled my room. It wasn't right though. Something didn't fit. My tired eyes strained to focus as I realised my room was a bright shade of purple. *Wake up, Aly.* I rubbed my eyes, but it made no difference.

I ran out to the garden and stood in awe as the sun flooded the sky with every shade of purple and fuchsia imaginable. The surface of the pool beautifully reflected the morning sky as I snapped a single photograph and proceeded to watch as the sky slowly turned blue.

By now, we all knew my sense of direction out there was pretty horrendous, so the thought of having to drive around a lot over the days that followed was daunting. I always had the thought that everyone would laugh at me. Maybe not to my face, but still.

As expected, sheering was exhausting. Nevertheless, it was one of the highlights of my time at the station. Long rides out on the quad bike for me and motorbikes for everyone else meant that my time there flew. I quickly got into my own little routine, so I'd be up and ready to help Peter drench the latest batch of sheep before pushing them out into their new paddocks.

It was brutal though. I never quite realised how rough this experience is for the stock. I suppose we all wear wool around our necks and on our feet and think they just sheer the wool from the sheep and then let them back to graze and wander. Perhaps my ignorance of the industry beforehand made the horror of seeing sheep fly down the chutes covered in blood and deep cuts even more shocking. How the shearers would violently grab and restrain them as they cut away at their coats before kicking them down the chute, startled and grazed.

As we drenched the sheep one by one, I would rub their heads, carefully avoiding any fresh cuts on their bodies. I felt extremely grateful for seeing what I did that week, however horrifying it was to see some of the stock get badly injured. I had lived a city life for over twenty years, and I started to think that my ignorance regarding the reality of these situations was something I needed to change. My trip so far had certainly opened up enough opportunities for me to learn and grow, something I wasn't taking for granted.

***

It was lonely all the way out there. There was no way for me to meet people. My friends had consisted of Lenor, Peter, Rob, Wally, Bolt, and Frodo the cat. I knew this would be the case before I ventured out here. It's the very reason why property owners like to take couples or two friends, so they can support and amuse each other in the middle of nowhere.

Lenor invited me out with her one Sunday morning to meet with one of her girlfriends. As it turned out, Lenor's friend needed some help over at her place, so we were discussing hiring people like me — backpackers! I didn't know anyone off the top of my head that needed work, but all it took was a quick post on Facebook, and before I knew it, a friend of a friend had contacted me expressing her interest. I passed on the details, and a few weeks later, MC arrived in Ilfracombe.

***

She had an interesting introduction to the Outback.

'Girls! I know this is a horrible job, but do you mind giving the bathrooms a quick clean and getting all the frogs out of the toilet?' Lenor asked.

MC's face was a picture. I didn't even flinch.

'Aly will show you everything. She is quite the master of getting rid of frogs!'

I beamed with an unusual sense of pride at my unusual skills.

I couldn't wait to show MC what happens when you flush a toilet in the Australian Outback.

Garbage bags in hand and a rubber glove for each of us; I posed next to the toilet like a professional giving a training session to her student.

'Now, I'll do the first one, and then you have a go, OK?' MC just nodded with a strange but excited smile across her face.

I pushed down on the flush and held my breath as green frogs fell from the toilet rim and swooshed around in the water. I manically grabbed at the little buggers and placed them in the black bag. I peered up at MC, her mouth was gaping open, and her eyes shimmered.

We continued to work on the 'frog dispensers', and it wasn't long before MC was a pro. Staring at her technique of quick and firm grabs, I wondered what had become of my life. Whatever had happened, I liked it!

As we continued to give the toilets a spring clean after removing all the frogs from their hiding place, we headed to the lake to free the little Freds.

'I'm not even allowed on the quad bike.' MC stated as I drove towards the water's edge.

My head shot up. 'What!? Why not?' I asked.

'She said it is too dangerous and she doesn't have insurance if anything were to happen to me.'

'Oh. Well, have you done much on the property? It can be hard work, but it's so much fun, and what an adventure!' I rambled.

'I don't really get asked to do much. I spend most of my time in and around the house helping out,' she mumbled, her head slightly bowed.

Shit. Here I was having the time of my life—racing quadbikes, flying planes, shearing sheep, driving utes all over the place and mustering. MC was left doing the gardening. Damn. Had I been taking my experience for granted? I was instantly filled with even more gratitude towards my host family. They really had given me a once in a lifetime experience—and for that—I cannot thank them enough.

***

I was only three weeks away from completing my eighty-eight days, and if I'm honest, I was saddened by the thought of leaving. Never before had I been this upset about leaving a place. Especially since I had been there for such a long stint. I felt at home there. I was learning so much. However, my journey had to continue.

Lenor had me painting the potbelly from the lounge. I took the fireplace piece by piece into the back garden and started to paint it back to its original coal black. Bopping away to my own rhythm, I heard the ute coming from a distance, followed by the door slamming and the gate squeaking.

'What ya doin'?' Rob startled me even though I knew he had just returned. Before I could reply with something sarcastic, as he could clearly see what I was doing, he laughed.

'Don't laugh. It's my work of art for the day!' I insisted.

'Well, you're doing great. I got something for you in the back of the ute. Picked it up on my travels!' He grinned and walked away.

'I'm not falling for that one Rob! No chance!' I shouted.

A dead kangaroo? A rotten pig? Rob enjoyed his pranks, and I wasn't falling for it this time. I carried on dabbing my paintbrush into the crevices of the potbelly.

Twenty minutes later. Lenor emerged from the kitchen with a spring in her step. 'Have you seen what Rob's brought you!?' she said, skipping towards the ute.

'Erm, no. I thought he was joking!' I said as I placed my paintbrush on top of the paint pot and ran to the ute.

Lenor pulled down the back, and my eyes slowly peered over the edge to see a small white face that was barely moving. I stepped closer as Lenor started to coo. A tiny little mud-splattered ewe lamb sat motionless on the metal tray. My mouth dropped. *Why didn't I listen!?* Lenor gently picked up the frail bundle of wool and brought her into the garden. I just stared in awe. I had no words, my heart melted. Lenor placed the little lamb on the ground, only for her to tumble and fall. Her knees knocked together; she hadn't an ounce of strength in her. My heart ached for the little creature.

We tried a couple more times to get her to walk only for her to stand completely still with her head bowed low. She was so tiny. My heart couldn't take this.

Lenor headed inside to find some powdered milk. I knelt down and slowly stroked the top of her head.

'Rob found her bogged in the dam. Must be from one of the neighbours' lots. Come on now little one,' Lenor said as she pulled the fragile lamb towards her and placed the teat in her mouth.

She struggled a little but eventually got some milk down. Whether it be a child or an orphaned animal, Lenor's mothering side always came out, and her experienced hands ensured that orphaned lambs were fed. Lenor slowly but surely tilted the bottle high, making sure she was taking enough in, whether she wanted it or not. With the dams drying up, this poor little darling must have headed towards the middle where small puddles of water remained, only for her to sink down into the mud, just like the 'roo I'd encountered before.

I stared into her large, glassy eyes and promised her that she would make it. She would be big and strong in no time.

'I can't get over how cute Layna is,' I said, squealing and prancing around the kitchen later that afternoon.

'Layna?' Lenor inquired.

'Yeah, I thought we could call her...Layna?' I said bashfully. I could feel my face turning red.

Lenor gave a smile that spoke a thousand words. Peter, Lenor and Rob all knew that you didn't name them. Once you name them, you become attached to them. With his little one being so young, weak and thin, there was a chance she wouldn't make it. But I promised Layna that she would be big and strong in no time, and I don't break my promises.

Rob was outside at the time, hacking apart a dead sheep in the garden that would provide plenty of meat for the months to come. As I watched him decapitate the carcass, I noticed Layna walk past the big pile of sheep limbs strewn across the lawn. I burst out laughing, making Rob jump. Bad timing on my part; he could have lost a finger! However, I found the image of poor innocent Layna watching Rob hack apart a member of her herd so bizarre. This wasn't right. I wanted to cover Layna's eyes; she was too young to see such barbaric behaviour against her fellow kind.

The following day Lenor had plans for a little golf, so I would essentially be home alone. With a few duties in my back pocket, I would look after Layna for most of the day.

I barely slept that night. I wasn't born and bred in the countryside. I could deal with death, but not when it was this close and this damn cute! She never made a sound that night. She just curled up with a belly full of milk and fell asleep.

Before I even turned the kettle on the next morning, I stepped outside to see little Layna stumbling as she got up on all fours and slowly walked around the gravel path. I spent the whole day attempting to feed her a bottle, but she wasn't having any of it. She would pull away every time I tried to get her to suckle. I tried again but with a bit more force. Nothing. She spent the day lying down around the garden, and I started to panic. *You cannot die. I can't take that*, I told myself.

I know I shouldn't have become so attached, but the deed was done. How could I not have fallen in love with a tiny gorgeous creature such as her? You would have to be a little cold, but I suppose that is what living in the bush and working with livestock does to you. It doesn't make you a bad person. It's just another defence mechanism. Animals come, and animals go.

I kept checking the time on my phone. *Oh please come home Lenor.* Layna got to the point where she was barely moving. She wouldn't drink milk or water.

After pacing the garden for the rest of the day, thinking about how terrible Layna must be feeling, I heard Lenor's car plough down the long driveway towards the house. *Yes! Thank God! Lenor will know what to do!*

Lenor took one look at my face and knew something was wrong.

'Layna won't drink. I've tried all day but she won't. I'm really worried! Her stomach feels rock hard, and she is all bloated! Isn't that a bad sign?' I started to become hysterical and just wanted to cry.

'Oh, don't worry. She will drink,' she calmly reassured me.

Lenor popped her head around the door and saw Layna slowly walk over to us. She went on to get her a bottle of milk. 'She might need it a bit warmer. Did you give it to her warm or cold?'

'Both!' I said, exasperated by my failed efforts.

'Her tummy hasn't had much food for a few days, so we will get it a little hotter and try and get her insides moving again. We'll give her a few extra scoops of milk powder too. It might give her diarrhoea for a bit, but at least she will have some goodness in her tummy for tonight.'

Just like that, Layna took to the bottle and made me look like a lying, emotional wreck. I was just happy to see her gulping the milk down regardless of who was feeding her.

Over the following three weeks, Layna recovered in leaps and bounds. She was no longer a shy, quiet little lamb, but she still had what can only be described as little mud-trousers on her legs. She would bleat at the top of her lungs every morning. She was constantly hungry for milk, loved to have her head scratched, and took a strange liking to toast.

She was getting stronger every day, but I still hated to leave her outside where temperatures got pretty low at night.

'Aly, she is a sheep. She has wool. She is designed to live outside, even in the cold!' Rob explained to me as he tried to stifle his giggles.

'Yeah, but, she is so *small* and doesn't have a lot of wool yet,' I pandered.

To keep me happy, Rob walked over to the pile of metal near the shed to find some chicken fencing to make Layna her own little hut to sleep in. I draped blankets around the wire mesh to stop any breeze from blowing through, and once I had popped her inside at night, I would cover it over with another blanket. However, most of the time she would hear my footsteps and poke her head up through the sheets, which was as comical as it sounds.

Not only was it ill-advised for me to become attached to her because of the chance that she could die, but on top of that, I was leaving. That was a cold hard fact. I tried not to think about it. I used the time I had left to love her even more and plan a way for me to slip her into my backpack before we left.

***

During the days that followed Peter was away, so we ploughed through the work that needed to be done on the property and around the house. Things had sure calmed down after shearing and workdays were shorter. I was fortunate to enjoy long two to three-hour breaks when the sun was high, so I would lay a blanket out in the garden and grab a book. Layna was always by my side. While I lay on my belly, she would walk over my back with her tiny hooves and head-butt my tummy, hoping to find non-existent nipples full of milk.

The wool on top of her head was thick and soft—perfect for digging my nails into and giving her a good scratch. After a good fuss, she would nuzzle up against my side and have a snooze.

When it came time to say my goodbyes, I held back the inevitable tears. Never before had I been so upset to leave a place. Normally my feet are so itchy I can't wait to get away, but here on this farm, I felt at home. You constantly hear nightmare stories around a box of goon in your hostel about backpackers being mistreated, underpaid or not paid *at all*.

I had well and truly landed on my feet when I met these wonderful people. Kangaroos dancing at sunset every night, and some crazy adventures. All in just eighty-eight days.

Those three months set me up for a wild ride in the land down under. I knew there was more to be seen, and I wasn't going to stop until I had seen it all.

I wasn't content just sticking to the east coast. Now that I had my second year approved, it was up to the rainforest and across to Darwin. Western Australia would be on the list too. I was liberated by the entire experience—cuts, bruises, and all.

Chapter Six

Journey into Arnhem Land

Cairns to Darwin. Australia, 2014.

Flight duration; two hours and twenty-four minutes. The clouds are beneath my feet, and my mouth is dry. As I sit on board the small A320, I'm constantly attempting to re-pressurise my ears. I'm Darwin bound with no money, no accommodation and no job. I'm falling into the hands of fate while at the same time deciding whether I believe in such a thing. Never before have I been so unprepared for the next leg of my journey. But years of travel will do that to you. It brings out the risk taker in all of us. Not for the thrill, but because letting go and seeing what happens, isn't always as scary as we think it may be.

If you told me four years ago to jump on a plane with $500 in my pocket, no job lined up, and no hostel accommodation sorted, I would have found the nearest cardboard box and hid in it. Most of us are terrified of the unknown.

Now take that uncertainty and stick it in a country 10,000 miles away from everything you know and love, and you have the beginnings of a true adventure. When you board a plane and have no idea what lies on the other end, you have to let go. Your mind lets go of the struggle. The struggle between wanting to feel comfortable and have everything planned, and craving the excitement of living on the edge.

Now, don't get me wrong. As a working holidaymaker, I know that breakdowns are no rare occurrence. You can almost guarantee that the person on the other side of the roof terrace in your hostel, who has her head in her hands and all hope sucked from her eyes, has either run out of funds or is about to. Maybe she can't find a job, and her bank balance has run into single digits? No job means no rent. No money means her dreams of continuing to travel are smashed. Travellers experience this every day all over the world, but how is it that so many can make it through the temporary struggle and keep on moving?

If I had a dollar for every plan I made that never came to fruition, I could buy the plane seat that I am sat in right now as I write this book.

Bump...bumpety bump bump.

'Ladies and Gentlemen, if you have a mobile device that you would like to switch on and is easily accessible without removing your seatbelt, it is now safe to do so.'

The whole plane, in sync, reached their right hand down between their legs into their bags, pulled out a shiny screen and sank back into their seats.

The night before flying, I had sent ten CouchSurfing requests out, apologising for the short notice and asking whether they had space to host me for a few days.

Declined. Declined. *Declined*!

My phone pinged a few times, and like a jewel on the screen, I saw 'Approved' with a phone number to call him once I had landed. I think I sank so far into my seat with glee that I was sat on the lap of the passenger behind me.

My only niggle of stress following this was finding a job, which happened the next morning. Not just any job either. A job so far from anything I might ever do again.

***

Just when I thought I had experienced the high point of my time in the Australian Outback, life knocked me back with a punch as if to say, 'Ah, ah, ah! You should know better than to think there isn't any more to see.'

Upon arriving in Darwin and exploring the city, I dreaded the idea of working again. I loved the freedom to move wherever I liked with whomever I liked.

Before arriving in Darwin, Scott and I had hit the road to explore Australia's East Coast. I made it a point to take advantage of this opportunity and see as much as financially possible. A highlight for both of us was Fraser

Island, the largest sand island in the world. We hired a bright pink 4x4 and kept our eyes open for dingoes. The beach became our bed, and my questionable driving decisions kept us literally on the edge of our seats. I made sure that I wasn't just working and saving the entire time. I knew that it might have been a once in a lifetime opportunity, so I was determined to enjoy every moment.

However, I was running seriously low on money, so I headed online in search of a bar job. Scrolling and scrolling every hour in hopes to be the first to respond to a newly added job post, I stumbled across an ad searching for a safari camp assistant! Safari!? Camp!? The job description didn't reveal much except this: 'Not for the faint-hearted'. Sounded like an adventure to me! This surely had to be taken, but my fingers dialled the number in hope.

What this job failed to mention was that it was in Arnhem Land, an aboriginal reserve in Australia's Northern Territory. I had only seen this place in documentaries. Entry onto the reserve required written permission from the council elder, who I would soon refer to as Henry.

I was told my main job roles were to help prepare breakfast and dinner, pack a lunch for the day and make a fire for the evening. The rest of the day was mine to relax on the veranda in front of the mirrored, albeit crocodile infested, Walker River. Or, if I preferred and the client was happy to have me, I could join along on their hunt. After the excitement of having a job in a place seen only in documentaries wore off, that little word kept replaying in my mind. *Hunt*. Their *hunt*.

What had I signed up for? I already knew I didn't have to shoot the poor animal myself, but I was a part of it somehow. This wasn't killing for survival. This was trophy hunting, an opportunity to show the world how (apparently) big your dick is.

Simon, the camp owner, wanted someone for four weeks but gave me the option to leave after the first week because it wasn't everyone's cup of tea. Aside from the fact that there was no internet or phone signal, decapitated buffalo heads would be dragged back to camp where it would be skinned, boiled, and the brain removed. I was starting to understand the job advertisement a little more.

From Darwin, Simon paid for me to catch the bus to Katherine and had pre-arranged to pick me up from there. Arnhem Land is accessible only during the dry season, and after a seven-hour bus journey, we still had to drive through the night, arriving at the chief elder's house around 8pm. Simon approached me like a bullet leaving its shell.

'Hey! Aly, right?' he quickly confirmed.

'Yeah, Hi, how ya doing? I'm Aly. Just got off the bus, obviously!' I said, trying to match his tempo but sounding like a complete moron.

'We still have to pick up some supplies from Coles and get some gas, but we will be on the road soon,' he said, as we walked with a bounce in our step over to the car park in front of the store.

I just tried to keep up, but for a short man, he sure could walk quickly. After grabbing some supplies, Simon asked if I wanted lunch because we had a long drive ahead. For some reason, whenever anyone I don't know asks me what I would like to eat I suddenly forget how to speak. *Food?* What's that? What food do I like, you ask? Erm. I like the edible kind. Chewable is my preference, but I can be flexible. I turned into a blubbering idiot when all I had to say was burgers, pasta or noodles. Such simple words escape me when I feel under pressure.

Conversation flowed, and I had a feeling Simon and I would get on really well, which was a big surprise to me. I had a fear that he would be intolerable. I feared he would be harsh and brash, cocky and arrogant. Bragging about his job like it was something to be praised. So far, I was wrong.

After munching down a bowl of Thai noodles, we drove to the petrol station. On the back of the trailer, a magnitude of jerry cans were squeezed on and tightly strapped down.

'Are you going to fill all of them? Why can't you use a barrel?' I questioned.

Simon's head bolted up, I could see the passion on his face as he spoke.

'Oh you could, back in the day. Now? Nope. Won't let you. I've had many an argument with them in there and higher up. Ridiculous. We aren't all bad guys. Some of us live in the middle of nowhere, y'no?'

I nodded.

'So, now I have to waste my time when I have better things to be doing, but y'no,' Simon continued.

After a seven-hour drive from Katherine into Arnhem Land, Simon took me to meet Henry, an elder on the reserve. It was late by this point, but I was very excited about conversing with such a high-standing indigenous Australian in his own home.

As I stared up at Henry's white curly hair, I was told all about the ceremonies that took place not long before I arrived. Men and women would be separated in secret for their own ceremonies and then brought together through dance and singing. It is their mission to instil their strong traditions into today's generation.

During our conversation, which went into their spiritual beliefs about the lightning God, members of Henry's family started hacking knives into a deep barrel. Curious as I am, I ventured over to see a dead dugong. It had been caught earlier and would be prepared for dinner that night. Welcome to Arnhem Land.

After saying goodbye to Henry and his family, we continued on towards Simon's camp. It was pitch black. There was no way I could get my bearings that night. It looked like there was nothing there as we pulled up to the campsite.

Simon showed me to my tent, where I curled up and instantly fell asleep.

I awoke to a cool layer of air wafting across my face as I lay on my uncomfortable single bed. I looked down towards my toes and saw the light blue tint of dawn streak through my tent. *Right,* I thought. *I'm here. Now what?*

My days would go as follows. 7.30am: Help prepare breakfast. 8am: Drink more coffee. Chat with the clients.

Everything was easy there. I told myself to just relax.

9am: Prepare lunch for the day. 10am: Say goodbye to Simon and the guests. 12pm: Do some laundry. Relax. 1pm: Start the generator. 2pm: Light a fire to heat the water for showers. 4pm: Start another fire for the camp.

Simple.

***

That morning as Simon and I gathered around the campfire, I watched a wallaby pass through the camp as I sipped slowly at my black coffee. I learnt more in that one morning than I had after spending months in the Queensland Outback. Simon wanted to quickly show me the generators, so he took me over to the master beast that powered the kitchen. Before we reached the metal-encased shed, Simon stopped and reached up to grab an overhanging branch.

'You see this leaf?' Simon asked.

'Yes.'

'See the black spots? This is poisonous to humans. Luckily, we don't go around eating leaves, but it's good to know!'

Wow, I thought. *This guy knows his stuff.*

Mornings at camp usually started in some magical way for me. Whether it was feeding Herbert, the hawk who perched majestically upon a high branch of a nearby tree or being treated to a miraculous show as flocks of cockatoos perched high, their yellow crests reaching as high as their screeching songs.

Breakfast was whatever the client wanted. Bacon and eggs were the usual favourites. The Americans couldn't resist it! I would throw the fatty bits to Herbert. Once, he took an entire pack of bacon off the table. Served me right for leaving it out. Well played, Herbert. Well played.

My first hunting experience came on my third day at camp, as I accompanied Simon and our two clients, Bill and Penny. After driving out down bush roads, we parked up in an open plain and set off on foot. Bows and arrows in the hands of our clients, I followed behind, wondering what would be in store for me that day.

After a two-hour trek through the scrub, not a single buffalo was spotted; we set forth to a large watering hole in hopes of spotting a large bull.

I didn't know quite what to expect on this venture. All I knew was that I wanted to take it all in. This was an opportunity to peer into an unseen world. I hated hunting. That was never going to change, but I wanted to talk to the people. Hear their stories. Hear the why's, where's and even how's.

After driving for around an hour and a half, we arrived at a native's home. Customarily, Simon informed the locals that hunting would be taking place near their property. Afterwards, I climbed back onto the back of the trailer with Penny and ducked my pelvis down so my head wouldn't meet any more branches as we followed a track through low-hanging trees. Simon and Bill were lucky enough to be sitting in the front, undercover. The ladies were on the back, open to the elements. That was fine. We were women—tough women. *Bring on the branches.*

Womanpower hurts sometimes.

The drive was exhausting. We were beaten by Mother Nature and had to fight off the biting weaver ants. We arrived at an opening and Simon briefed us on the hunt. We were to stay close. Most importantly, we were never to separate from the group.

We trekked through the bush for around two hours. There no buffalos, not even a young one, so we stopped for a break. Weaver ants covered the trees, and Simon educated us on their citrusy taste. If they bite you, bite them back.

So I did. Wow. All I needed was some gin to wash down the lemony taste, and we had a party.

Penny had her bow ready. Today was her turn to have her first-ever kill. Bill said he would wait until tomorrow. They spotted their target, but stayed low. The wind wasn't right. It would take our scent right to the prey. We had to circle around and hope the wind didn't change again. Simon and Penny crept towards the buffalo's strong hindquarters.

Up until this point, I wasn't enjoying myself in the way my companions were. I just didn't get it. Sure, there was an instinctual adrenaline rush, but we have evolved. They weren't killing for survival. They were killing for a trophy. Penny and Simon stooped down around 100 metres in front of us. Bill and I hung back, hiding within the trees. Their target stood just over 120 metres from them. A challenging shot, even for a professional with a bow.

Suddenly the wind changed, and the mighty beast spun around and stared right at them. My heart skipped a beat as I saw the bull begin to charge towards them, before falling a mere 30 metres away from Penny's feet. She had fired directly at the buffalo's chest, piercing its heart. Simon said that the bull had died before he even knew what had happened.

Comforting? This animal was dead. Lying at our feet, soon to be hacked apart, the head and cape taken to hang above the fireplace. It would become the centre of conversation, and friends would look at it with awe and admiration. *It's not a sport. She shot a defenceless animal.* I just didn't get it. I still don't get it.

We ended the hunt with beers and conversation around the campfire. What a way to spend the day. That month turned out to be very interesting. Whether I agreed with it or not, I was learning. I kept an open mind and asked a million questions. Already, I was so glad I had taken that job. Little did I know what was to come.

***

We bid farewell to Bill and Penny as we waited for our new client to arrive. This one was going to be different, wanting something more than your average buffalo. He wanted more than the well-trodden tracks surrounding Simon's camp. He saught a prize buffalo, and he was prepared to go far out into the bush to find one.

We would end up being the most isolated people in Australia. FACT.

You are here to learn Aly, so ask some questions!

'So, what is it like to send a dead animal's head through customs?' I was blunt, genuinely interested in the procedure.

'Takes years!' Carl said. 'It took four years to get every part of my elephant through. Nightmare.'

Simon took another sip of his beer as my heart sank into the depths of my stomach. *Elephant?* My hands started to shake. *How many animals has this guy killed?* In a way, I felt hypocritical for feeling differently because it was an elephant. Should it matter what animal it is?

'Some fucks back in Africa messed up. I got my tusks, but I thought its foot was a goner. Cheats and liars they are; you can't trust them to get all the parts to you. Most of them pocket the best parts for themselves,' he continued

I'm sorry, are you taking the moral high ground over those people who stole one of your fucking dead animal parts? Are you somehow better them? Did you honestly just complain about someone stealing your elephant foot? Do you

really not see the issue with what you just said? I can't take this.

Adrenaline pumped through my system at a rate of knots. My body flinched when I tried to look him in the face.

Why did I find the company of Bill and Penny far more pleasurable than this person's? They were both hunters. Both took pride in shooting an animal and posing with it. Carl interrupted my train of thought.

'Aly, if you ever come to the states, you can come and stay at mine. You would love my animal room!' he boasted.

Would I now? What on earth makes you think I would enjoy that? Have I not been clear enough with my thoughts and opinions on this? Normal human beings have TV rooms or sometimes game rooms. Animal rooms, though? Fucking hell.

I tried to keep very quiet through most of the conversations that took place. It was the only way I could bite my tongue. It is not like me to bite anything and hold back how I feel. The blood inside me was simmering. It was only a matter of time before it came to a boil.

The campfire conversation shifted from elephants to lions, to crocodiles. He boasted a lot about how he had 'collected' the 'big five' in Africa.

'So, you've killed a crocodile too?' I asked.

'Yes mam. Almost took my face off. Funny story,' he chuckled.

Took his face off? Finally, a story about hunting I could listen to. I straightened up and took a swig of my beer.

'Now, I didn't know this at the time, but crocs don't always die instantly! You can't approach it immediately just in case you missed, or the shot wasn't lethal,' he started.

Simon just nodded his head; he understood the crocs better than most. If you shoot a one, you must wait to make your approach. If it isn't dead, you will know about it.

'Long story short. I saw this beautiful 17ft beast on the bank. It was just taking in the sun, y'no. They don't move too much then. Shot it, BANG. Perfect!' He laughed and congratulated himself. 'The black fellas told me to hang back for about six hours! Six hours? I was like, what the hell man! Till they explained. So we stuck around in the heat till the afternoon, and this thing had not moved a muscle! We get in the boat, and once we reached the other side, we got the cameras out. Seriously, this thing was fucking huge. The head was like that!' He gestured with his hands.

Simon just nodded, and at the same time, I was thinking, *Yep, we know where this is going.*

'So, I climbed onto its back and my legs would barely fucking fit over the body. Man, they are *huge*! Anyway, I smiled, and the fucking thing only swung its head out and tried to grab me, throwing me off at the same time. The black fellas had to drag me away! It weren't dead. It weren't dead! Incredible!' he claimed.

Incredible indeed.

Prick.

***

Before we set out, my morning routine was standard. There were just a few loose ends to tie up before we embarked on the big bush hunt. This hunt wasn't attempted by Simon very often. Maybe once every three to four years. It involved entering parts of Arnhem Land where even the Aboriginals do not enter, or even know how to navigate. It would drive us out through thick bushland into No Man's Land. We took supplies; tinned goods and dried food. But for the rest, we would live off the land. I'd stay at base camp and prepare dampa while the men set out on the quad bike with the bows and guns.

'Are you alright back there?'

'Oh yeah!' I shouted just before a branch smacked me around the face. *I'm just dandy.*

Creepy crawlies are a common sight in Oz. Spiders, lizards, flies and moths. But when someone who lives out in the bush—who lives and breathes wilderness— jumps from the jeep quicker than you do, you can only imagine what dropped on him.

Ants.

Not any sort of ants. Weaver ants. I'd enjoyed their citrusy taste previously, but having an entire nest of them crawl all over you, biting you everywhere is not fun! We would smack each other wildly while pulling our clothes off in a frantic attempt to rid our bodies of them.

***

The following morning brought a heavy dew. The fog hung low on the scrub, and every particle glistened individually. We packed up camp and headed closer to better water, where we would stay for the remainder of the hunt.

The overgrown scrubland provided many challenges in getting from point A to B. To counter this, Simon, as he does every few years, would burn off the scrub to allow new life to grow. Every few miles, he would lean out of the jeep, lighter in hand, and start a fire.

We were twenty-four hours in, and we'd had no trouble up to that point. However, upon approaching the midpoint of our journey to better water, the terrain got rough. I mean *really rough*. Then, like a nightmare reaching its climax, we heard the dreaded sound come from the front of the jeep.

Pssssssshhhooooooooooo.

Our first flat tyre. Thanks to ironwood. Not bad going considering that we had been driving for a day and a half and hadn't had to change once.

Continuing on, fresh tyre all secure, we travelled through creeks and over more scrubland. We were ducking and weaving in the back to avoid getting covered in weaver ants or losing an eye to a pointy twig. We lit more and more fires.

The wind was higher that day, the terrain seemed drier, and the dead grass seemed taller. The fire was roaring and crackling not far behind the vehicle, consuming whatever lay in its path. Then suddenly, all we heard was BANG, *psssssssshhhhhhhhoooooo.*

My heart stopped. The screech of the breaks seemed to slow time. The crackling fire behind us intensified.

There was no time to change the tyre, so we drove it to the rim and pushed on with three wheels. As we came to a halt, I was put on lookout as they fought to get another spare tyre out from under the quad bike, which had been wedged onto the trailer.

I positioned myself 50 yards from the jeep. Another 100 yards in front of me the smoke danced with the warm breeze. Orange flames were spreading to my left and reached the eucalyptus treetops in seconds. I froze watching the fire jump from one tree to the next, to the next and the next.

I calmed. The fire was heading away from us.

Then, as though the flames could read my thoughts, a gust of wind hit my face, and what was once a smoke cloud in front of me erupted 15ft into the air. The fire was raging; gobbling the oxygen it had just been supplied.

Fifty yards from the jeep. Fifty yards from the fire.

All I remember in that instant was how Simon had taught me how to burn off an area for a safe campfire, using a green leafy branch to extinguish the tiny flames. I could only imagine the size of the branch we would need now.

I stood motionless, watching and listening as the flames got closer and closer. The whole time I was planning an escape route.

No matter how beautiful the scenery was at our new campsite, my heart wouldn't calm down. I could still feel the searing heat against my skin.

Where Is She?

***

The fire was still raging in the surrounding area as we retired from the campfire and entered our tents. I could hear large crackles and snaps all around the camp.

I fell asleep. Somehow.

What seemed like seconds later, I awoke to burning amber enveloping my sleeping bag. Quickly, I jumped out and started beating the tent with my fists, but there was no stopping it. It was everywhere. The crackling deafened me as the fire consumed everything in its path. At that moment, I felt a coolness on my face and heard the birds sing me into the day. I bolted up and looked around at my sleeping bag and pillow, perfectly scrunched around me.

That night, and for the following four nights, I dreamt of fire.

The following morning brought no dew. I lay shaking, listening to the cockatoos squawk on the river bank. Then, something woke me from my dwellings of fire and destruction; a huge splash resounded, and the birdsong ceased. We had ourselves a crocodile.

I called him George. He later became known as Boy George. He was curious, but he was small. A 4.5ft long freshwater crocodile. On the first day of camp along the beautiful river, he would follow me. I was probably the first human he had ever seen, and he didn't quite know what to think of me. However, once he saw my size as I stepped forward on the bank, he swished his tail and was gone. The next few days consisted of reading, wandering through the bush naked and making dampa. George would visit occasionally, and I was very appreciative of the company.

By day five, I realised I had not looked in a mirror since we left base camp at Walker River. My hair, which swung down around my waist in gentle waves, was softer than ever. My legs were covered with cuts, bruises and bites, a map of my journey over the past few days. I have never been an overly vain person, but on that day, I touched my face and decided I needed to see my reflection. It could be found only in the river—if I was brave enough to lean over for long enough, which I was not. Occasionally I would feed the fish some day-old bread and take water to wash some clothes, but that was about it.

The following morning, we packed up camp and headed back to our halfway point, around six hours away. After driving 400 yards, we noticed that the fire we had set the previous day had burnt out just outside our camping zone. Another hard slap to affirm the dangers of fire, which you never truly appreciate until you are caught in one. I had been promised that driving back would be easier through the burnt out planes. However, nothing could have been further from the truth. Jet-black ash kicked up from all angles and into my face.

The sun was setting fast, and we had lost some coordination, so we camped up on the other side of the river where we stopped five nights previously. Simon escorted me down to the water to check out the surroundings and make sure it was safe enough for me to bathe and return to my natural skin colour. We navigated our way through grass that stood taller than both of us. I carefully placed my feet into the footprints of Simon's shoes. My eyes darted left and right, as did Simon's. We were risking a nasty encounter with a slithery reptile in this long grass, and this was the first time I started to question my faith in Simon's decisions.

We emerged from the other side unscathed, but my return trip back through the long thicket weighed heavily on my mind. *Help is so far away. It's getting dark. We are in the bush. You do not mess around with the Australian wildlife out here.*

My anxiety quickly shifted direction as we approached the water. The billabong was dark. Eerie. Still. The low-hanging branches gently tickled the water's surface but refused to submerge into the darkness.

My feet carefully navigated over the rocky water's edge, but I refused to take my eyes off the still surface. *Please don't be deep. Please don't be deep.*

'Wow, now that is *deep*. We definitely have company,' Simon said, matter-of-factly.

Damn it Simon, what did I just say!?

He was right. The water was practically black, and these lands were swarming with crocodiles. Simon looked at me, and then with his eyes, did a panoramic sweep of what can only be described as a swampland. He turned back to me and said something I will never forget for the rest of my life.

'Looks a bit croc-y, but you should be OK!'

Looks a bit croc-y, but I should be OK? Is that what he just said to me?

I have never stared so hard at water in all my life. This was the perfect home for a man-eating saltwater crocodile.

Simon grabbed the small bucket I had in my hand and took to the water's edge. 'I'll get your first bucket. Do you think you will need more?'

'Nope. Nope. Nope.'

'If you do need any more then make sure you look about *there*,' he gestured with his arm, pointing out around a metre in front of him. I stood a few metres behind. 'If there's a croc here and he wants me, he will be about there. He could be looking at me right now. Water is too damn dark to see it anyway.'

If it were scientifically possible, I would say my heart had stopped just then. Simon crouched down in front of me, looking ahead into the dark water at all times. He slowly dunked the bucket under the calm surface, causing a ripple to form around his hand. My heart started again, this time it was pounding. *Oh God. This is bad.*

If we did indeed have company, they certainly knew that we were there now.

It's amazing how one small bucket of water can remove multiple layers of black ash from your skin, but only if you feel your life is being threatened by a giant crocodile.

My time was almost done, and the rollercoaster of a month was fast approaching its conclusion.

***

An inner conflict was raging from the moment I heard about the position in Arnhem Land. I had an image of hunters and how they would act, talk, dress and think of themselves. I *knew* hunting was wrong but had never even seen a single documentary on hunting or spoken to an actual hunter. Why?

Was I so terrified to allow others to expand my mind and challenge my beliefs? I was so confident that hunting was a barbaric act that I thought there was nothing more to know. It was black and white. All hunters are animals, and it should be banned for eternity. The more passionate I became on the topic, the more my mind closed.

What *I* believed was correct. What *you* believe is a lie.

Arnhem Land did two things to me. It confirmed even more that hunting is barbaric, but at the same time, it contradicted my beliefs. It challenged me, and I let it. *I let it.*

I could have just gone, been bitter and resentful of the activities around me and cut out the need for conversation, all to preserve the thoughts within my own head.

Then it hit me. Whatever I believed, the job was an opportunity. It stood right in front of me. Should I have slammed it closed? Should I have screamed, 'Everything behind that door is wrong and evil even though I have never been through it in my life? I just know it's true because *I* said so!'

I took a chance and opened my world to an utterly new experience. I had walked through the door.

My beliefs and knowledge regarding hunting changed and expanded. My passionate stance and beliefs regarding hunting still remained, but now they were covered in notes and edits and the answers to the questions that I had about it all.

Your mind is limitless. When you start to explore and question your beliefs, some may be confirmed and reinforced, but some may be drastically altered forever. Open your mind and allow life to smash apart your current values and beliefs. Accept the challenge and grow from it.

It could be something simple. For example, I have two beliefs. The first one being that our taste buds change throughout our lives, and secondly, I hate avocado. However, these two beliefs challenge each other. One day I chose to ignore my limiting beliefs, and I tried a piece of avocado. At this point, I could have still hated it, which would have been fine as long as I was 100% open to the experience. However, I actually really liked it. In fact, I loved it! Whatever the outcome, it's more knowledge, more power, and more experience to pull from later.

The more our minds fill and overflow, and the more lessons we learn, people we meet and beliefs we challenge, the more our individuality grows. Let your opinions and thoughts on issues broaden as a result of your experiences. Never be limited by what you *think* you know. Form your own standpoint on the world. Have novel thoughts on situations and say them with conviction. Talk to people and actually *listen*.

Chapter Seven

Little did I know

Western Australia. December 2014.

Views from either side of the bus encapsulated rural Australia, miles of scrubland as far as the eye could see. Yet again another contrast to Perth's immaculate cityscape. After my escapades in Arnhem Land, Scott and I jumped on a $99 flight to Bali to have some well needed time together. We sipped cold beers in Ubud after long days on the back of a hired scooter, chasing the sun, passing rice paddy after rice paddy.

We ventured out to the Gili islands, where we cuddled cats on the beach and regularly refused the very open offering of weed from bar owners. We started our days chasing turtles amongst the reefs and ending them on a beanbag outside a beautiful bamboo resort that graced the coastline.

After exploring Lombok, we headed back to Bali, where Scott would witness me get absolutely paralytic. A well-known water park offered tourists from all over the world white-knuckle water slides and an excessive amount of liquor at their pool bars. After slipping and sliding down almost every slide we came across, we headed to the bar for a couple of drinks.

An Aussie couple who were sipping cocktails and building up their already tanned bodies introduced themselves. After a little bit of small talk, Scott went off with her husband to play water polo, leaving his lovely wife to coax me into multiple cocktails known by many and remembered by few, the Long Island Iced Tea.

No matter how hard I attempt to remember what happened next, my mind only takes me to events that happened hours later when Scott returned to find me rather inebriated.

'Act sober, or they might not let you on!' Scott whispered as I clambered up the steps to our favourite water slide, suppressing a drunken giggle.

Following multiple successes on the slides, Scott decided it was probably best to get me some food, so we headed out to a street lined with fast food restaurants and convenience stores.

'Do you want a KFC?' Scott asked while trying to keep me vertical on the side of the road.

'Nooooo. No. Let's get something from the shop,' I mumbled.

We picked out some Pringles and other assorted snacks before heading back out into the sun to hail a cab back to the hotel.

'Aww, Scott. Scott! There's a KFC right theeere! Why didn't we go to KFC!?' I grumbled, swaying madly from side to side.

Scott, defeated and exasperated, hailed a cab. From that moment on, this story has become a staple at social gatherings, and well, at any moment Scott can squeeze it into the conversation.

After spending all my money on Bintang and hippy pants, we headed to Perth for a week or so before Scott had to leave as his visa was almost up. I needed to get myself back onto Gumtree to find my next paycheck.

***

After several hours driving north of Perth on the air-conditioned Greyhound coach, we stopped for a twenty-minute break.

As I wandered away from the petrol pumps, I spied a long, big cage full of parrots and cockatoos. How odd! How many service stations do you stumble across with a miniature zoo? My eye was then caught by something bigger than the bird mansion and much shinier. A stunning road train with two loaded trailers tailing behind it pulled up alongside our coach. More for my dad than for me, I whipped out my phone and snapped a photo. At the same time, I saw the driver inside the cabin. I blushed and gave him a thumbs up in a way that said, 'Hope you don't mind me taking a photo of your big shiny truck because I have already done it and yeah...'

He waved me over through the large, angled windscreens.

'D'ya want a photo with the truck?' he enquired.

'Yes please!'

I explained that my dad was a truck driver from England and that he would love these photos. After a quick photoshoot, he jumped aboard and honked his enormous horn as he powered on and left the service station, making it suddenly feel so much bigger.

***

We passed through Port Dennison. The first sign of civilisation for hours. I suddenly halted mid-thought. And there are two sheep on the balcony of that house...I really am going back into the bush.

As I saw signs gracing shop windows with the name of the town engraved above the establishment. I grabbed my backpack and walked towards the front of the bus as the driver pulled up to the side of the road.

He turned to me, 'Where are you going?'

I was taken aback for a moment and muttered my stop.

To which he nodded and smiled, and I disembarked the coach, full of beans and curiosity about why it sounded so unbelievable to the driver.

According to one of the few emails I received from my new boss, the hotel should have been just across the road from the bus stop. It was not across the road from the bus stop. I looked right and saw a red tile building down the way with the word 'Tavern' painted across the tiles. I then looked to my left, while rolling a thin cigarette, to see a corner hotel. I had googled the building before leaving Perth so I would have a faint idea of what to look for, and it looked about right.

This town was neither the smallest in Australia nor the largest. With a population of less than a thousand people, it offered those passing through the quiet, serene country town view you expect from Australia. But because of my experience with these kinds of towns, I was looking less at the small, quaint shops and more at the people I would have to deal with while intoxicated. Them being intoxicated that is. Not me. Even though I have been known to take the lead behind the bar when showing people how the British drink.

The 'main street' included a church with beautiful gothic architecture that dated back to 1936, a small post office, and a visitor's centre run by a lady with shoulder-length hair and thin-rimmed glasses that I would learn was wonderfully friendly. There was the usual IGA,

Red Cross shop and then dotted in between were small shops selling beautifully crafted handmade bits and bobs, and mainly B&Bs. I'm sure you are thinking the same I was—this town is wild.

I tugged my backpack up the wide road and took in as much as possible. No one here looks out of the ordinary. Smells nice. Greener than I thought it would be.

Not too many thoughts occurred within the 50 metres I had travelled, but I was feeling positive. My backpack and I just squeezed through the entrance to the bar. TAB machines lined the right corner where an indigenous man stared hard at the screens. A gentleman sat on a bar stool drinking a can of lemon squash, and only two young people from Perth who had apparently broken down were occupying the other end of the bar.

After a short while, a short, thin girl with a smile as big as the sun appeared from the other side of the bar.

'Can I help you?' she said.

'Hi, yes, erm, I'm starting work here today?' I said as I gave out a nervous laugh.

'Oh!' she exclaimed! 'You must be Alyshia?'

'Yes, but call me Aly.'

'Great, I'll go and grab Robert.'

While I waited and chatted with the two young people from Perth about my travels, they told me how brave I was for travelling alone, and I consoled them on their car situation. I heard, 'Hi Aly!' and I spun around too fast, my backpack almost taking me down like a lead brick.

It was not Robert. Unless Robert was a handsome, tall, blonde woman with beautiful hair and a confident smile. And breasts. It was Karen. As I said, she was a tall, slim but well-built woman with thick blond hair and eyes that made me feel instantly at home.

Robert, I later discovered, was neither blonde nor tall. He was a wanker.

Karen showed me to my little room upstairs. Long corridors jutted off here and there, and I suddenly remembered that this was originally a hotel. Guests now stayed around the back in small cabins, and the upstairs was for staff only. My room was just big enough for a double bed, a free-standing rail and a side table. Best of all, it had air conditioning. I was set.

Following a quick tour of the building, I had a couple of hours to relax before she wanted me to help out at the bar. They had a lot of tables for dinner, and there could be a rush.

There was no rush. I had seen deserts busier than that bar. But alas, 'twas a country pub.

No matter how many bars you have worked in, the only thing that takes a bit of time is getting used to the tills/prices. After a few shifts, you get your groove back. Working alongside Sara, we battled through the four people at the bar like champions. I made one mistake on the till, forgetting it was time for happy hour prices.

I was pouring wine like a pro, but I'd had a lot of practice.

One fellow named Darren was of particular concern, as he was clearly heading for the floor in the near future. Sara and I had agreed that enough was enough and that we would cut him off.

'Can I av anova drink?' Darren shouted, slumped over his empty bottle.

'Nope darling, sorry,' I replied, waiting for his reaction to being cut off.

Darren responded to this in a less than courteous way, throwing a 10-cent coin at Sara and called her a 'fucking bitch'. He did however, leave the pub, and he did understand why we wouldn't serve him. Probably because he just got chucked out of one of the other pubs in the town.

Later in my shift, I quickly formed my opinion on Robert the wanker. I witnessed two events that night that told me why the entire town couldn't wait for him to leave. Now, before I continue, let me tell you this.

Robert was very lovely to me when I arrived, and we had some nice chats over the bar during my first, short shift. However, on the whole, he was a wanker. The first time he revealed his true self was when he noticed that a glass bottle of dry (ginger ale) was by the spirits section.

He turned to Sara.

'What is this!' he said in a low, stern voice while holding up the half-empty bottle.

If that was asked of me, I would have had to tell him it was a refreshing beverage which people like to mix with spirits such as Scotch.

Sara explained that someone wanted a Scotch and dry. Obviously.

'Well, when someone orders that, you give them the bottle and you charge them for the whole bottle! How am I going to make money from this! I'll have to pour it down the drain! That doesn't make me money! And you never use coke from the cans as a mixer!' he shouted as he walked towards the cold-room, appearing a second later with a bottle of coke.

'You use a bottle, OK!?'

Sara was silent.

'You hear that?' he exclaimed as he untwisted the lid to let the gas out.

'Yes, it means it's still-'

'It means the drink is still fizzy, OK!' Robert spat, cutting Sara off.

I looked around. A lady on the other side of the bar looked on in horror. Rule number one of running a business: keep your staff happy. *Never* belittle them and shout at them in front of customers. I just hoped he kept his customers happy and didn't reveal his foul temper to them.

I was quickly proven wrong.

About an hour into my shift, a young European-looking couple entered the bar. They were from Switzerland and in between grabbing them a Corona and a SuperDry, I found out a bit about their journey through Australia so far. The two beers amounted to $16.40, and they wanted to pay with a card. I directed them over to the EFTPOS machine, and Robert quickly snapped behind me.

'NO, NO, NO! Go to the ATM machine we have right there!'

'But it charges us $4 to withdraw,' the Swiss lad replied, slightly startled.

'I don't *care* what it charges you! You're not paying with a card!' Robert boomed.

The smiles they entered the bar with quickly faded from their faces. I felt my cheeks burning. I was embarrassed for them. I quickly understood why they sold the pub and why the whole town was waiting for him to leave.

I knocked off after two hours and let Sara finish with the six customers we had left.

***

My first day off was approaching, and everyone at the bar suddenly asked what my plans were. It could have been general interest, but the way their faces lit up, it was as if they had an offer up their sleeves. In a good way. Karen told me that the locals would take me out. I found out that they really felt sorry for the barmaids. They knew we were backpackers with no mode of transportation and they didn't want us sitting around upstairs going insane.

'What ya doin' tomorrow, Aly?' Andy enquired while sipping his drink.

Well, I have a business meeting at two, and the gardener will be coming around four...

'Not much,' I said bashfully

'Fancy coming out on the Jet Ski? It'll be an early start, mind,' Andy warned.

You have a Jet Ski!? Jeez. I can always remember watching teens race around in the sea on those things back when I went on holiday with my parents. It had always been on my bucket list, so I didn't hesitate to take him up on his offer.

'Cool, well, be out the back around seven.'

***

The clear salt water splashed against my face as Andy spun the Jet Ski left and right. I smiled as my fingers grasped the sides of his life jacket. As we went further out, smashing into waves and being thrown into the air laughing, my mind couldn't process the scenery quick enough. Beautiful cliffs, white sand, no people. Such a contrast to my east coast journey.

Andy was ready to take a wave head on and told me to brace myself. As we hit the wave, my feet lifted from the Jet Ski, and we crashed back down harder and quicker than we flew up. Both silent for a second, Andy looked over his shoulder, and we both burst into laughter. One thing was for sure—we'd be walking like John Wayne for a while!

***

As I stood under the gushing water, washing off the sand and salt of the morning adventure, I came to realise just how much I would miss this land of contrast. Sure, I chose a job that required dealing with rude and arrogant drunks until the early hours, but the handful of wonderful people I had met outweighed the negative aspects.

James was another regular. Super chatty and loved to play *Budapest* on repeat throughout the night. Whether we raced through the open valleys at 160km/ph on the back of his Harley Davidson or we drank beer at his place with a few of the other regulars, I could always rely on James to put a smile on my face. However, no matter how many wonderful souls I met, no connection would be stronger than the one I made with Sharon.

Sharon was the cleaner at the pub, and she was fucking fab. After she knocked off from her shift, she would make her way to the bar and have a couple of drinks to keep me company.

At first, Sharon, or Shaz as we all called her, could come across as quite intimidating. She had such an air of strength and no-shits-given that you never knew what would come out of her mouth next. I could relate to this completely. I think this is why we got on so well.

We spent Christmas together at Michelle's (Shaz's friend, who I also fell in love with). We'd have drinks at hers, and I fell head over heels for her dog, Maverick. Shaz was a real friend and someone who I would soon owe a lot to.

There was hope where I thought hope was lost. When I was in Blackall, I hated the idea of ever having to work in a country town again. Sure, it was tiny. The hours were long, and not much went on, ever. But I was able to make connections with people I will never forget. The good, the bad and the ugly. Each of them made this tiny town special to me.

***

'Why don't you look at flights to come home?' Scott asked one evening over the phone.

'Why?' I asked.

'Well, with all these big plans we might not be home again for quite some time. It's almost two years since you have seen your parents, so it would be nice to come for a visit.'

We had been discussing our future travels in quite some detail lately. Being in such a small town, I wasn't really able to spend my wages, so I had been putting away $250 into my savings every week and for the first time in a long time, my bank balance was looking healthy and our future, exciting!

'I'll have a look at cheap flights later tonight' I said.

'Are you excited to finally visit Thailand?' Scott asked.

'I'm buzzing! After hearing you talk about it so much, I just want to jump on a plane right now! First I just have to get through these final few months at the bar!'

South East Asia had been at the top of my bucket list for so long, and through earning and spending continuously in Australia, it felt like I would never have the money to do it. The bar may have been quiet, and the pay may have been questionable, but it was finally all coming together. *Let's just get through the rest of my time here and hope there are no hiccups along the way.*

***

Karen told me not to listen to hearsay regarding the pub being sold.

'I'll tell you right now Aly, so you don't hear it from anyone else. We have sold the pub, but none of you will lose your jobs over it.'

Karen was right—it was all anyone could talk about. The rumours were hilarious. *Apparently,* all the bar staff would indeed lose their jobs, and nobody could wait for Robert to leave. Then as the weeks passed and the assuming 'hand-over date' was constantly looming, the locals started to doubt whether the pub would ever be sold.

I have to say, I was thrilled at the idea of a new boss who didn't look over our shoulders, waiting to pick our every move apart.

Plans to make an alfresco area were exciting, knocking out through to the back with decking and an eating area. After almost two months of the mundane shit, finally, some exciting stuff was happening.

I was really enjoying my time behind the bar, but I had yet to meet the man that was the subject of every conversation at the time. He was a local apparently, but not many knew his face or name.

This all changed one weekday afternoon when I served a round-faced man with dark hair a Bundy and Coke. I really wish he had introduced himself before asking what I thought about working there.

'Urgh, y'no. It's alright. It's a colourful place to work at times. Not very challenging. Pretty boring most of the time to be honest! Sometimes you don't see punters for hours on end, and there is only so much you can clean!' I rambled away, thinking he was just another local enjoying his favourite spirit.

A man that was sat next to him interrupted with, 'So when are you taking over then?'

Fuck. Really? Fuck, fuck, fuck!

I sulked away into the background. What had I just said to my soon-to-be boss?

Idiot.

I pulled down all the spirit bottles and cleaned the shelf, again.

A week or two passed before we met again. The rumours were spiralling out of control at this stage, and even I started to believe this hand-over would never happen.

His visits became much more frequent after this. Meeting with Karen and Robert to sign paperwork, or have a meeting, or discuss legal matters. I have no idea what they spoke about in that little office out back. All I know is that he really liked his Bundy and Coke.

After every meeting, he seemed to sulk to the bar area to have a few drinks. He was rather pleasant, and chitchat extended to changes he was making to the pub and not much else.

One evening, he came in for dinner with his two daughters. Two young teenage girls, very pretty, enjoyed a large Outback meal with their father. When it came time to settle up the bill, he told me to try a bit of the food.

'Why?' I asked.

'It's pretty fucking terrible! Try it. Seriously. I don't want to say anything but...' he whispered as he leaned over the bar.

'Do you want me to tell the chef?' I enquired.

'No, no, no,' he whispered.

'At least tell Karen. I don't think she has any idea of how crap he can be at times,' I said.

He signalled me over to the other side of the bar and asked, 'Do you work on Thursday?'

I reeled off my shift time, which I knew by heart but still double checked on the roster behind me. Thursdays were a good day. Split shift with Emily. We alternated each week. This week, I was on from opening time until four.

'Cool, well I'll be in tomorrow evening if you were in the bar and fancied grabbing a drink!' he asked.

'Sure. I'm normally around somewhere. I'll pop down for a couple no doubt, around six-ish.'

Morning shift on a Thursday was as expected. Slow. Monotonous. Same old same old. The following day was Friday, a big day regardless. Punters always came in for a big blow out.

Better not have too many drinks tonight. One or two and then an early night to...to what? Have another boring night? Fuck it, live a little Aly. You've survived hangovers before. Pound a couple of Panadeine with an extra-strong coffee in the morning and you'll be good.

I finished my shift, pulled off my work clothes and flung on my summer dress before heading down to the bar.

Little did I know that ten hours later I would be taken to the hospital in a police car. That my life would be changed forever.

PART TWO

Chapter Eight

000

My fingers dialled the three digits without a second thought.

'Police, ambulance or fire station?' the operator fired off my options.

'Police please,' I stated with a strange sense of ease.

'What's the emergency?' the woman asked.

'I was raped.' The words left my mouth like a blunt bullet hurtling into the atmosphere

'OK, where are you now?'

I gave my address.

'Are you safe? Is the offender still with you?' She went through her mandatory questions.

'No, I'm safe. I'm with a friend. He isn't here.'

'OK, I'll have an officer out to you in less than twenty minutes.'

I sat on the balcony. The tiny police station could be seen from the pub. I stared hard up the road, waiting for movement.

Chapter Nine

Screaming

I couldn't breathe.

It was as if a hole had been punched through my chest. The previous hour's events suddenly dawned on me. My heart exploded and I grabbed my chest with my fist as I gasped through pained, stifled cries.

I tried to hold it in, but I couldn't. The nurse who sat at her desk next to me stared at her screen, holding back the urge to envelope me in her arms.

My breathing became rapid and my mind span with intrusive thoughts.

The white clinical room started to collapse around me as my breathing became deeper and faster. I couldn't scream. All I could manage were muffled gasps for air while I dug my nails into my chest hoping to slow my racing heart.

No. The only word racing through my head. *No. This hasn't happened to me. This can't have happened to me. It's a bad dream. A really bad dream. I need to wake up.* I searched the room for any signs that it wasn't real, but everything steered me to the same conclusion.

During my panic, a young doctor entered the room and took a seat next to the nurse. I couldn't stop. My heart kept racing against the drumming thoughts in my head I was trying to silence. A slight scream passed my lips as I battled to calm down.

My eyes locked with the young male doctor's. 'I can't! I'm sorry! I'm sorry!' The words rasping against my throat as I searched the room for anything familiar that could ground me. There was nothing. Two pairs of eyes I had never seen before and a room I had never visited.

OH GOD! I needed to scream so badly.

My lungs felt like they would collapse in on themselves if I dared to try. I craved a face I knew. I needed someone there right then that I could hold. At that moment when I thought the world as I knew it was imploding around me, I was so alone.

Chapter Ten

Inside

I sat in that small room for seven hours. I was visited by doctors, nurses, counsellors, investigators, police officers and detectives.

My body was photographed. I was cold. I sat there with no underwear, in a thin summer dress, turning blue from the air conditioning. My mind started to retreat into the darkness. Across those seven hours, my mind packed up its belongings and set my state of consciousness to standby.

A small cup of pills was handed to me by yet another new face.

'Basically darling, we have here the morning after pill, something for chlamydia...' My mind spun again with the heavy reality that was sinking in as she listed off all the diseases I may have contracted.

At that moment all I could think about were the words that the detective branded into my head.

'There is a very good chance this won't go to court, or that he will even be charged. You need to be prepared for that.'

I nodded as she continued to tell me that the man who raped me might very well get away with it.

'I worked a case not long ago. Went on for two years. We had all the evidence. Father, sexually abusing his three children. It was a slam-dunk. There was no way the jury could give a not guilty verdict,' she stated before pausing and looking me straight in the eye. 'The jury went out for ten minutes. Came back with the verdict of *not guilty*. We couldn't believe it, but that's how it goes. We had acres of evidence, but it wasn't enough. The jury is told that the evidence must show beyond a reasonable doubt...'

I started to zone out as she calmly explained in many different ways how unlikely it would be for me to get any justice.

'Consent. It's one of the hardest things to prove in a court of law. There is very little evidence in these cases. It's horrible. It's wrong, but it's how it is. One word against another.'

The words swirled around my cortex like a storm as I lay back on the examination bed, parting my legs as the nurse slid on a pair of gloves.

'Open your legs a bit more, darling.' My nails were digging into the soft bed. 'This won't take long, I promise.'

The nurse stopped. She tried but failed to hide the look of amazement on her face. I knew what it was.

Alyshia Ford

I was wearing a tampon that night. It was there, wedged high against my cervix. She prepared the evidence, placing it inside a bag and then walked over to my side.

'That could be your saving grace in court, darling.'

Chapter Eleven

The Right Words

After spending seven hours in the hospital being poked, prodded, photographed and questioned, I awoke in my bed from a dreamless sleep. I sat, burying my head into my pillow, wailing into the phone. Scott was on the other end, in just as much shock, trying to find the right words to say. There were no right words. There were 10,000 miles between us, and all we wanted was each other.

My phone lit up, showing a message from Shaz. I ignored it.

Should I tell her?

I needed to get out of the pub. Anywhere would be better. I typed out the words on my phone before quickly holding the backspace button. I did this multiple times until I realised it would never look right on the screen. I hit send and braced myself as my phone started to ring seconds later.

Shit.

'Go and tell Karen and Robert that you are coming to stay with me. Pack a bag. I'm coming over.'

Just like that, a woman who knew me for two months dropped everything and came running to my side. She offered me a bed, but I took the sofa. I couldn't lie in a bed, not yet. The feeling of the sheets against my body and the empty space beside me terrified me to my core.

I was to do what I needed to do. If that meant sleeping on the sofa, then so be it.

Chapter Twelve

Nothing

My eyes opened just enough to allow light in—to remind me that I was still alive. I felt nothing else for the rest of the day. I didn't move. I lay there, listening to the subtle sounds of Maverick at my side. A slight scratch along the floor. An exhale through his long nose. There was a moment when I forgot. It was short-lived.

I pulled myself upright. The sofa was my safe place. No one could hurt me there. My eyes fixed to one spot in the room, but I don't remember what I saw. I couldn't tell you the time at which my body woke me. I wasn't panicked. I wasn't frightened. My body held my brain where it always sat between my ears.

I question now whether anything was happening up there. Silence. No flashbacks. No intrusive thoughts. Nothing.

I don't know which is worse. To feel everything, or to feel absolutely nothing.

Chapter Thirteen

Help

Aly: **12.41pm:** *I want to feel again, but my mind won't let me feel. I'm dead. He killed the part of me that lets me know I'm alive. I can't speak yet. I'm screaming inside. I can't move, but all I want to do is run away. I have support, but I need someone who knows me. Who loves me. I want to be wrapped up and finally, let go of my pain. I need someone to whisper me to sleep and tell me it will all be ok. I'm not Aly anymore. He killed Aly. I don't know who I am anymore.'*

Daniel: **13.50pm:** *Sweetheart, I can't begin to understand how you feel and I can't deny or object to anything you have written above. I CAN be completely devastated to hear that this piece of shit has 'killed' Aly. Aly can't be dead. Not at his hand. She is hurt, she is scared, and she is a little lost, but she IS alive. It is OK that she has retreated, but she will be back. She has to be. Give me a call as soon as you are free and feel up to it. Spoke to mom. She suggested the same as me, that you come stay here for a bit. I know a girl who can meet you in Perth and stay with you at the airport until you get here to me, or I can fly over and pick you up.*

Aly: **13.59pm:** *I'm scared, Daniel. I've never been so terrified in all my life. The police are running late. They will ring me when they get to the station. I'll ring you after that. I know nothing more. For all I know he will be at the pub when I return to collect my things. It's only a matter of time till* people in town find out. Then they'll take sides. Then I'll have to leave. I have no idea what I'm saying. I haven't muttered a single word today. I'm just moving my thumb over the letters in hopes that I will start to feel something again.

Daniel: 14.03pm: *I've a friend in Perth. I'm going to see if she can drive me to Northampton. Either way, I'll be there in the next few days.*

Aly: 14.11pm: *I don't know what to say. In any other situation, I would say no. But not this time. I'm not going to be good company. I may just cling to you. I might just scream on your shoulder. But I need someone to bring Aly back. It's a five-hour drive from Perth. Sharon said she has plenty of room for you to stay here. I can't believe you are going to do this.*

Daniel: 14.16pm: *If it is what Aly needs, it's what Aly's friend will do. She is more than worth it. Ask the police today if you can come back with me. Let me know, and I'll get you a ticket. Will see if my friend can turn around and drive us back to Perth for a flight. We can fly back when we need to.*

Aly: 14.18pm: *Could you stay for a couple of nights? I need to get my test results. There is a bus to Perth from here. If not, that's OK. I'll see what the police say.*

Daniel: 14.18pm: *Of course I can.*

Aly: 14.22: *If I could cry I would. Thank you.*

Daniel: 14.24pm: *There is time for that later. Now, just stay as strong as you can.*

Chapter Fourteen

Darkness

'I have a couple of friends coming over today. They come every week. They are always helping me around the place. They must look at me and feel sorry for me or something!' she said, smiling through tender eyes.

Shaz tried to make conversation with me. Her kind words and concern were evident, but I lacked the emotional availability to show gratitude.

'If it is too much then I can tell them to come by another time. It's not a problem sweetheart.'

I forced some words out. 'It's fine, really.'

The truth was, I didn't care. I focused back on my invisible spot and drifted back into the darkness.

Mavericks' howl pulled me back up to the world above. It was followed quickly by the sound of tyres tearing their way up the drive. I stared through the curtain that was blocking my view. I leaned forward to try and show some sign that I was alive. As Sarah put her head around the door, a smile spread across her face.

'Hiya! I'm Sarah!'

'Shaz is just in the shower,' I replied, expressionless.

Her face dropped. The lines at the corners of her eyes smoothed out, and her smile faded.

'Are you alright?' she asked, startled.

What? What did I say?

'Yeah. I'm fine,' I lied.

Not exactly a big lie. I no longer felt fine, or distressed, or exhausted. But you can't respond with 'I'm nothing,' can you?

A heavy-set man, presumably Sarah's husband, said hello as he walked straight into the house. Shaz met him in her towel. They laughed, and she told them she would be out in a minute.

'Are you OK darling? They are really nice. Have they said hello?' Shaz's voice bubbled up from behind the sofa.

'Yeah, they seem nice.'

Apparently, it doesn't take a rocket scientist to tell that I am not OK.

'What the hell happened to her?' I hear Sarah ask Shaz.

Apparently, my emotionless response raised alarm bells. After a few brief explanations, Sarah entered the house slowly, kissed me on the side of the head and walked away. Mommy instincts activated. Sarah's husband stayed outside most of the time. He didn't want me to feel threatened.

I don't remember much from my time beneath the surface. Words that were directed at me brought me out briefly, but not fully. Just enough for me to respond and keep them from worrying too much.

'It's OK, she's not here. She's not with us right now, but she'll be OK.' Shaz's voice entered briefly but powerfully through my floating body as she sat behind me, discussing whatever happy normal people discuss with their friends.

No. I'm not here, and I'm OK with that.

My peaceful lull was broken at the sound of my phone ringing.

Private number.

That meant one thing. I had been waiting for that moment for what felt like forever. The detective wanted me at the police station to complete my statement. Hours of monotonously talking and discussing every single detail of that night lay ahead.

Everything from the shape of the wine glass to the feeling of him forcing his way inside me.

Chapter Fifteen

My Statement

The station was a ghost town with only the detective, Shaz, and myself to occupy the area. Papers scattered the walls with lots of reference codes, names, and police jargon. Every employee had a very tight, cramped area in which to work. How many crimes actually got committed in this small town was a mystery to me. Then I remembered I wasn't exactly screaming about what happened to me from the rooftops, so perhaps more than I thought.

The darkness kept pulling me under. Every time I tried to pull myself up to the surface I had to relive the event in more detail than I cared to remember. My mind pushed that night deep within my subconscious. My body felt numb when in reality my mind was working overtime to protect my conscious self. If your body cannot handle what has just happened, your mind helps you to escape. Like morphine, coursing through your veins, your body remains numb. Completely immobile. Through this paralysis, you're contradicted at every turn, hyper-aware of your environment. If your mind were an army, it would disregard anything but danger.

The moment any trigger is pulled, you feel your pupils dilate and your neck crane upwards.

The evening in question was combed through methodically. Every detail. What drinks did I order and at what time? Did I order them? Or did he? Who else was in the bar? These were the easy questions. I estimated times and gave her my best recount of the evening's events.

'Right Aly, that's really good. Would you like to take a break? Next, we have to move on to the actual event, and that could be really hard,' the detective spoke softly to me.

Shaz stayed inside as I took myself out for ten minutes.

As she finished typing out the rest of my statement, I listened to the rhythmic tapping at the keyboard and stared hard at the desk. Her desk was crowded with items, yet I am unable to recall a single one of them.

Shaz pulled up to the local IGA supermarket only to be faced with a closed sign. *What? How long had we been in the police station?*

Unbeknownst to me at the time, it had taken several hours to get a full statement, because I kept drifting off and spacing out.

Did I?

This freaked me out because I specifically recalled talking slowly but with ease, without huge gaps or breaks. Apparently not. I had completely disassociated myself. The detective voiced her concerns with Shaz, asking how long I had been like this. I couldn't even answer that myself.

Chapter Sixteen

Run

Bile gurgled in my stomach, and my heart started to pound as I lifted myself up from my safe place. I'd only grabbed a handful of things from my room before coming to Shaz's house. I had to go back. I had to leave the sofa and my world beneath the surface and re-enter that building.

Karen and Robert were told I would be coming, and *he* was told to stay away from me.

I'll go into my room. Pack. Leave. He won't be there. No one will be there. I can go through the back. I can see Emily. It won't take long.

My racing heart was the first thing I had felt for over seventy-two hours, but it only served to deepen the numbness.

I sank into the ute and Shaz began to drive back towards the place I never wished to enter again. The pub should have felt fairly safe. The pub is not where it happened, but he could be there. My eyes darted rapidly in all directions as we crossed the limits of the town. I was frozen but alert. My brain instinctively looked for any signs of danger.

He was near. A building site full of his workers was situated just behind the pub car park. He was seen there today. What if he was watching me?

Get inside.

Shaz took me up to my room, and I locked the door.

I slowly sorted through my possessions, not caring what I kept and what I threw out.

It felt like it was taking an eternity for Shaz to finish her shift, so I let myself sink back down.

A knock on the door brought me back out of the abyss.

'Aly, it's me, Shaz,' a beautifully calming voice reassured me from the hallway.

I unlocked the door and saw Shaz holding a plate of my favourite meal, reef and beef. She made me promise I would eat something. I said I would try. As I stared down at the pale pink prawns, I remembered that this was the last meal I ate at the bar just four nights ago. I stomached a bit more, for Shaz. Not for me.

Since the event, food had barely passed my lips. I couldn't stomach a single bite. Though I forced down little from my dinner plate each night, in all honesty, it wasn't for my sake. In reality, my body must have been screaming so loudly for some sort of nutrients, but my mind failed to notify me of the pain in my gut.

I wanted to smoke so badly, but I was frozen with fear in that room. *He could be here. If not him, then someone.* I didn't want to see anyone. I wanted to stay in my deep, dark pit of emptiness without anyone else to ask how I was or look at me like a broken doll.

I held onto the doorknob and slowly unlocked the overpainted heavy door. Like a meerkat within the long grass of the Savanna, I peeked my head out and checked my surroundings for predators. I tuned into every creak and sound, sight and smell. After what felt like an hour, my instincts told my physical body that it was safe to move.

I crept towards the end of the hallway and surveyed my surroundings one more time. I looked to my left towards the wide balcony where you could see the entire town, and they in return could see you. I stopped. I couldn't go out there. I looked right and saw a half-opened door to a smaller balcony around the back of the pub.

I continued to creep, slowly picking up my pace, passing the table where my nice coffee still sat. Past the top of the staircase and on to the outside.

Gathering my things, I headed downstairs with Shaz at my side. Karen was stood at the bottom looking me dead in the eyes.

'I know this is hard, but will you be coming back or not?' she asked nonchalantly, stunning me out of my abyss, causing me to almost drop the few belongings I was holding.

'I need to know whether you are coming back or not because if not then we need to find someone to replace you,' she continued. Her tone was cold and harsh.

I was searching for words as I tried to make sense of what she was asking, and why she thought it was OK to ask such a question after what had happened.

'No. I'm not coming back,' I said in a colder tone than hers.

Karen was a mother. A grandmother. This event threatened their plans of selling the pub and the blame lay at my feet. She looked at me like a broken barstool, wondering if I could be fixed or if I would need to be replaced.

I sat panicked in the ute, waiting for Shaz with Emily at my side. Emily was the first person I told. Knocking on her door, I entered, words hurtling out as I stared at her tired face. She sat by my side as we waited for the first police officer to pull up, and she was behind me as we stormed towards the hospital.

'I have to pick up a few things from IGA and the chemist. Do you want to come in with me or wait in the car?' Shaz asked.

'I'll come in.'

'Really? You sure? You don't have to darling.'

I wanted to. I knew that it would be good for me, and I knew Shaz would be at my side if I was to encounter any regulars, or even worse, *him*. To be honest, the idea of staying in the car terrified me more. In the car, I had nowhere to run. Only my hands to hide my face in if anyone who recognised me passed by. I was better out of a metal box.

As I stepped into the tiny local pharmacy, my heart began to race. I couldn't run in here. I felt boxed in. *Breathe Aly. It's OK. He won't come in. He won't. You do not need to worry about this. Just look at the cosmetics. Focus on something else.*

Shower gels. Face scrubs. Nothing interested me. It was all mundane. Pointless. I didn't need it.

As I glided around the shelves, my line of vision turned to a basket of nail polish. For a moment, I was stolen by a memory. A simple, sweet memory of my childhood where I used to look through the reduced nail polish and make-up to see what I could buy with my pocket money.

I quietly fumbled around and pulled out the winner. $2. OK.

'I got something,' I said, quietly showing Shaz my purchase. 'I thought I could do my nails tonight. I used to love doing that.'

'Yeah! Absolutely!' Her eyes said more than her words could. Hope was returning. It's as though that tiny bottle was a stepping-stone into my recovery. A token of self-love and care.

Chapter Seventeen

Daniel

During the day, when Shaz went to work, I was alone. I peered into the tall food cupboard to collect some coffee and sugar. Shaz had a place for everything, and everything was in its place. A saying my mom drummed into me whenever she saw my messy room as a child.

My days were filled with waiting, waiting for calls from the police, and then nothing but emptiness in between. Today the waiting would be for two arrivals. First, the detective would be making an appearance with her superintendent, as I had to sign an amendment for my statement.

Maverick's howl notified me of their arrival. I stupidly left the gate ajar, so he bolted outside towards the officials. I had met Maverick only a handful of times prior to coming here five nights ago, and in that time, he was yet to leave my side. He slept by the sofa throughout the night and at my feet during the day. He never left me.

'Maverick!' I painfully whispered, unable to scream or pull him away from charging at the car, full of protection and love.

I called him a few more times as they stepped out of the car, pulling at his collar to calm him down.

'Have you ever spoken to him on the phone?' the superintendent asked me as we all took a seat around the table.

My heart stopped. *No. Why? What? Did he say I did? I'm confused.* My head spun for answers

'Do you have his number?'

'No. Never had a reason to.' I said.

A flash of disappointment flooded their faces as they exchanged glances. *What was happening?*

'That's a shame. Something we can do, but would never push on you if you didn't want to, is for you to call him.'

Call him? What? Why? My heart was beating against my chest so hard I thought it would burst. The room started to spin, and I thought I was about to lose consciousness and fall into the darkness.

'Don't worry. Really. It's just an option. We would be able to bring you in and record the conversation so you could get him to confess over the phone and we could have some evidence to take to court. But really, you don't have to.'

'No! I *can't*. I'm sorry!' I cried.

I can't. There is no way that was going to happen. Why would they ask me to do that?

'Either way, we are hoping to charge him in the next two to three days. We just have to get some more statements from people who saw you that night,' they explained while packing up the white papers around them. 'What are your next moves? Planning to leave anytime soon?' they asked.

'My friend is landing tonight in Perth. He should be here tomorrow. He is going to take me back to Melbourne after my doctor's appointment if that's OK?' I mumbled.

'Of course, not a problem. Just make sure you can give us your new details wherever you move to so we can keep in touch, OK?'

As the car reversed out of the property, I let out a long breathe. I was exhausted.

***

I could spot Daniel speeding past the property in a small white hire car. Nothing like the cars people drove around here. It could have been no one else.

We drew a rough map for him the previous night to help him find Shaz's shack from the main highway. I gave it two minutes until he realised he had gone too far and turned around further up the gravel road.

The sparkling white car pulled up to the front of the house, and my heart sank.

'Maverick, get here!' Shaz shouted across to our loyal guard dog, who hadn't let a man near me in four days.

I squeezed between the child gates so the dogs couldn't follow me. My eyes drew a straight line from my feet to his face as he jumped out. A single look can speak a thousand words, but I had none to offer. I stood motionless. Numb. I sensed his level of caution as he threw his shirt back on from the back seat before approaching me.

Our eyes met, and he let out a single, pained sigh until he reached out his arms and I collapsed into him. For as long as I can remember, a hug could bring forth a thousand tears from me. But now, nothing. He held me for a while until I pulled back and just looked him straight in the eye. Not a single word had passed between us.

I noticed sadness forming in his eyes, as though my lack of emotional response made it harder for him to see me like this. We embraced once again, maybe more for his sake this time.

Chapter Eighteen

Melbourne

As we approached the Jetstar check-in desk, I cowered slightly behind Daniel, nudging him silently to take the lead, which he did. Over a week had passed and my mind, for the most part, remained absent. For days I had tried to trigger myself to feel something again. I couldn't take the numbness anymore. I had to feel again.

Be careful what you wish for Aly.

I knew the emotional waves would come when they were ready, but it felt so inhuman not to feel.

My efforts to trigger myself fell flat, barely breaking through a handful of times. I was able to hold better conversations, but in reality, I still remained silent the majority of the time. My mind was not ready to handle reality yet, and I had no choice but to go along on this dull and mundane ride.

'Hi, we are both booked on the flight to Melbourne, and we would like to sit together if possible,' Daniel said.

Darren, the tall, thin Jetstar employee smiled and took our passports to check us onto the flight. My eyes darted everywhere. *Please say they have a half-empty flight,*

so I don't need to be near anyone. Why is this taking so long?
I started to form a plan for how I would deal with sitting next to some random stranger when Darren interrupted us.

'Well, we have nothing together, but I can put you both on an aisle seat so you would technically be next to each other?' He relayed what his screen was saying.

'Thing is, I am flying Aly back to Melbourne with me as she was sexually assaulted a few days ago. She really doesn't feel comfortable sitting next to anyone else,' he said quietly while leaning over the counter slightly.

'Right, I see,' Darren said, glancing at me, his eyes screaming with sympathy. 'Let me have a look,' he said, as he continued to type away at his hidden keyboard.

It still felt like I was watching a TV drama of a character's life play out in front of me. The words didn't penetrate me, and no emotion was felt. It was as though I was stood in an empty room watching every action play out on a stage. I had no connection with the characters, and no urge to relate to what was happening. Nothing.

'What I can do is I can put you both in the seats where the crew would normally sit, and they will sit in your seats. That means you will both be alone and together. Would that be OK?' he said with growing concern in his eyes.

'Sure, yes, thank you,' we both said.

Does that mean we will be facing everyone? We will both stand out like sore thumbs, surely? The cabin crew seating is obviously not near the other passengers, but everyone can see. They will wonder why on earth we are sat there. I didn't want anyone to look. I just wanted to get out of there. Regardless of my initial anxiety, I praised Darren to the highest as we moved through to the departure lounge.

We took a seat near our boarding gate for only a few minutes before our waiting was interrupted via the intercom.

'Could a Miss Alyshia Ford and a Mr. Daniel Wood please come to the check-in desk? Would a Miss Alyshia Ford and Daniel Wood travelling to Melbourne, please come to the check-in desk. Thank you.'

Our heads sprung up like meerkats. My name had never been announced before. *OK... Now what?* We headed over and saw Darren standing behind the quiet counter smiling at us.

'Hey guys. What I have done is I have managed to clear a row of seats for you by moving some people around so you will have some privacy! Could I grab your tickets and give you these new ones?' he chirped.

A warmth spread across my chest and into my heart. As he passed us back our tickets, I tried to look as deep as I could into his eyes. I wanted my gratitude to pierce his soul.

'Thank you, thank you so much,' I strained through watery eyes.

As I squeezed into my seat next to the window, Daniel sat on the aisle, giving us space to relax. I fell back into a numbness that I had just previously forgotten about. You would expect to have these great waves of emotion, leaving a place that held such pain and fear. Happiness? Relief? Sadness? Nothing. As we ascended into the clouds, I felt very little about leaving this side of Australia. As we descended towards Victoria, however, my numbness took on a whole new meaning.

Suddenly, I felt like a lost little girl who had strayed away from her parents at the supermarket. I had been to Melbourne twice, and right by my side was a man who wouldn't let anything happen to me. So why did I feel so lost? I didn't want to go to Melbourne, but I didn't have a choice. Did I? I didn't want to stay in or anywhere near that town. I wanted to go to Melbourne and stay with Daniel, but everything happened so quickly, it felt as though I was a broken vase being transported from A to B to get fixed. I was conflicted. Tears filled my eyes as I saw the city beneath us. So many questions and emotions that I could neither answer or explain. This new world was penetrating my numbness, and I was terrified.

Daniel's sister had arranged to pick us up from arrivals, which caused my stomach to knot. I had already met Carlie on my previous trip to Melbourne. She was lovely; there was nothing wrong with her, but she was another person that might want to make conversation with me. The idea of contact, making small talk, smiling, all to please someone else, made me want to run and hide. Not like they would have asked any of those things from me; but it is what you do, right? I have been taught my whole life to be polite to others, smile, and say please and thank you.

Daniel took the back seat with the little ones, which I was eternally grateful for; even on a good day I can't take children, never mind on a day when I could barely say hello to a grown adult. I jumped in the front with Carlie, and apart from a few pleasantries and a smile, she never forced conversation on me. I tried to muster some energy before we arrived at Rita's house—Daniel and Carlie's mom that is. A beautiful, crazy and wonderful woman who had opened up her home to me for as long as needed.

After a quick hug and confirmation that our flight was pleasant enough, I took my bag to the spare room. I dumped it down and stood staring into the abyss. It felt light and freeing, everything I needed at the time. I was so exhausted after so much small talk that I just wanted to close the door and collapse onto the bed. Needless to say, I didn't. I went and sat out in the lounge and tried to be the polite girl I was raised to be, smiling here and there, adding very little to the conversation.

This was going to be my home for a while. A place to heal. This is where I had to find Aly. I had to find where she was and understand how to get her back.

Chapter Nineteen

Floating

I loved Aly.

Aly was so bright, energetic and full of life. She was ambitious, always working on projects and teaching herself new things. Travelling the world and learning everything she could, wherever she was. She made friends so easily. She moved around rooms with ease and could chat with anyone. She was strong. If she didn't like someone, they would know about it. She was feisty. Straight down the line. Wouldn't suffer fools easily.

She had it all planned out.

I love Aly. I wish I could see her. She would know how to make me happy. She would know what to say and what to do. She would help me heal. I don't know where she is though. I lost her. I'm scared she'll never come back. She was my best friend.

That's the hole inside of my chest. That's what's missing. Everything that made me Aly. I'm missing her. He took her that night. He destroyed her. He didn't know how taking that part of me would kill me. I'm dead.

I walk with no direction.

I act with no purpose.

I don't see a future. I don't see what tomorrow will bring. I don't see what the next sixty minutes will bring.

Where Is She?

I'm floating aimlessly through this world in a bubble that is all mine. No music. No soundtrack. Just floating.

I can't taste food. Aly used to love food. I don't care if my stomach hurts and screams when it's empty. I eat enough to stop me from passing out.

I have no purpose anymore. I'm scared by this. When someone has no purpose, they cease to exist. I can only exist if I can get Aly back, but she is gone.

My eyes do not see the world like Aly saw the world. I see a chair that I can sit in. I see a shower that will make me clean. I see a car, but it is outside of my bubble, so I don't care about the car. I don't think about the car. I don't think about the chair. I don't think.

I'm floating. Floating above a girl who is crunched on her side on the edge of a strange bed that's illuminated by a TV show. The characters on TV see. They see what is happening to this girl, but they are in a glass bubble. They can only watch from a distance. They do not stop it. They cannot stop it. They are the only witnesses to this event.

Her awareness travels to the place she is too scared to think about. He is there too. He likes to be there. He stays there. Having fun. She wants to die, but she is already dead.

She floats through this world watching herself. No emotion. No feeling. Because a dead girl can't feel. She can only float.

Nothingness.

Chapter Twenty

Rita

I don't quite know how to hold myself in this new environment. How high I should hold my head even though the world was pushing down on my neck, making it impossible to look up. What do I do with my hands when they are empty? Where and how should I sit?

I slowly debated what conversation would be suitable or required in this circumstance. I was a stranger in this home. I walked in broken. How is one meant to act towards such gracious hosts, when all I want to do is bury yourself under the duvet and ride out the storm?

'Don't feel like you need to stay out here with me, Aly,' Rita spoke as though she was reading my thoughts.

'No, it's fine. Really. I want to.'

Our eyes stayed locked on one another as though we both decided on our next move.

'I just wanted to say thank you for letting-' I started.

'No. Don't say a word. You are more than welcome here. You stay as long as you need. I won't hear another word on the matter,' she said.

I bowed my head in acceptance.

'You know, Aly...' Rita started as she fingered the armrest of the chair, looking down at her lap. 'I have been through quite a lot myself. Daniel wouldn't have told you, and even he doesn't know everything.'

Rita had been through more than hurt in her life. Every word of her story felt as though it was more painful for her now than ever. Anyone could see how uncomfortable it was for her to tell this story, and through every word, I felt closer to someone, who only ten minutes ago, was almost a complete stranger.

'I let it consume my life, Aly. Don't let it consume yours. Talk to me. Talk to Daniel. Please, do not keep this inside like I did.'

'Have you ever spoken to anyone about this other than your family?' I asked, already knowing the answer in my heart.

'Never. It's too late for that now. For me. I have held onto this my entire life.' Her eyes filled with defeat.

'Thank you, Rita.'

I have always been a talker. Looking back on my life, it has probably been the trait that has saved my sanity through my darkest days. I confide in those around me and rarely have a problem talking through my issues. At that moment, I didn't know how to express how I felt inside. Explaining to someone that you feel absolutely nothing one minute and then apologising for a random outburst the next is unsettling. All I hoped for is that they would get to see the real Aly soon and not this floating body with no facial expression.

Chapter Twenty-One

Dead

Please, someone, tell me how to get her back. Please, someone, tell me that she will be coming back. Life isn't worth living without her.

I feel like I am mourning her. My best friend is dead, and there is nothing I can do to bring her back.

I am not Aly anymore.

She is dead.

I want her back.

I can see her in a garden. She is running. Skipping. She can smell the flowers. She is smiling such a big beautiful smile. She laughs. She has everything.

Aly was murdered by that man.

I can't feel. Aly can feel. She felt everything. She can't be gone. Aly is my soul. My soul has been taken. I am now a walking body. Walking dead. Without a soul, I shall continue to float and walk around this planet. Without Aly, I cannot heal.

If she is not dead, how can I prove that she is not dead? How can I make myself believe that I am not dead?

Chapter Twenty-Two
The Call

The previous night had been my first without any medication to aid my sleep. Probably because I was exhausted from cleaning all day, which was good.

However, this led me to wake up with awful anxiety. My heart was pounding. Not at first. I didn't feel strung to the bed in chains, but it developed quickly, within about ten minutes, around the time I started making my coffee.

I gave up on the coffee and decided to clean Daniel's room. It just needed to be done. This made me more anxious because I did it without his permission, I felt so terrible. I was so scared that he would come home early and be angry with me. Looking back, this was ridiculous.

My phone rang. Private number. It was the detective, but I felt no hope in my heart. I had been disappointed enough as of late. I answered.

'Hi Alyshia. This is Detective Michelle Browning. How are you?'

She sounded rushed? Busy? There were some voices in the background. She sounded like she was moving around people.

'Alyshia, I just thought I would let you know that we have charged him today.'

I dropped to my knees and raised my left hand halfway into the air. An iron weight slowly lifted from my shoulders.

Oh, if only I could have been a fly on the wall while they told him he was charged. I had been dreaming about this moment for two weeks, imagining it playing out in my head. So why didn't I feel better? I was expecting to feel amazing. Elated. Free. Prancing around the living room shouting hallelujah. The reality was very different.

I was happy. Don't get me wrong. To hear that the system was taking my side on this, that was a huge step towards justice. But it didn't change anything. The pain didn't suddenly disappear. The experience and memories were not erased from my past or present. While it was a small victory, absolutely nothing changed for me.

One emotion I took from the call was relief. Prior to this all happening, I had no idea how many people get away with rape. Forget getting it to court—even getting a person charged with this crime is extremely difficult. How can you prove consent? It's one person's word against the other. Unless you are beaten and bloody, or there were viable witnesses to the event, there is no way to prove you didn't consent.

A harrowing realisation is that, without a doubt, sexual assault is the easiest crime in the world to get away with.

Chapter Twenty-Three

Allie

Other than Daniel, the only friend I had in close proximity was Allie. She was one of the first people I met back when I arrived in Melbourne. I joined her on the concrete floor of the hostel and listened to her strum on a guitar. Seeing Allie caused me very little anxiety. However, getting to her did. I knew deep down I had to do this. I had to push myself out of my comfort zone and face my anxiety head on.

Frustration hit when I found that the things that came so easy to me before were now major struggles. Catching a bus. Stepping out of the house. Walking down a crowded street. Every step made my heart pound harder, and somehow I mustered up the determination to roll with the pain in my chest.

It will be good for you, Aly. The longer you stay inside, the harder it will become to return to normality. I accepted the anxiety and went for it. Repeating to myself that I was safe. *He isn't here. I'm OK. He doesn't know where I am.*

Headphones in, I tapped my Myki card to the reader and took a seat next to the window. I jumped on Facebook and asked Allie if it was OK to message her until I arrived. I quickly realised that I wasn't so much afraid of people as I was of places. My experience did not seem to taint my expectation of those around me; more so just being alone. On the other hand, there were only a few people I could actually bare to be around. I wanted their company. I craved it. But not strangers. Not new people.

The ability to navigate the streets of Melbourne came back to me as I headed straight towards Parliament house, not looking at anyone, just gripping my phone and taking it step by step.

You can't maintain a flight or fight response for too long. My anxiety faded into the background, and I instantly became exhausted as I stood waiting on the concrete steps. My brain went into overdrive as I tried to absorb my surroundings. Unconsciously, my eyes darted across the scene; much like an antelope hearing a rustle in the grass in front of her.

Across the road from where I stood, I spotted a pair of round-rimmed sunglasses over a friendly smile. It felt like it took an eternity for her to cross the road.

***

'What d'ya want to do?'

Allie was the perfect person to be around; she could read my face and see that I didn't have a clue which way was up, so she took the lead.

'How about coffee from that cute place, a takeaway. We could go and sit down in that little park thing with the water feature. God, I have lived here for how long? No idea what it's called, but it's over there!' she pointed through the newly crowded street.

'Yeah, great,' I squeaked.

Great? More like perfection. Coffee and a quiet place. This girl knows what she's doing.

We grabbed our tiny coffee cups from the barista, who was as hipster as they come and clearly belonged in Melbourne. Allie eyed a quiet, grassy area for us to relax in. At that moment, walking past a hundred strangers brought zero anxiety, mainly because I was caught up in the moment, doing what two gals do when they are catching up after a long time apart.

I decided to lie down on my side with my arm propping up my head as we chatted about all sorts of stuff. There was never any pressure to talk about what happened. Even though I did tell her eventually. Up until that point, I felt slightly at peace.

The moment didn't last too long, and my heart rate soon returned to dangerously high levels, but that moment of peace existed. I felt it.

I didn't notice it at the time, but looking back I know that I experienced normality again. It was possible. More possible than I had cared to think about during that time.

Baby steps, Aly. We'll get there.

Chapter Twenty-Four

Trial

8:30am. Too much was going on that day. I didn't want to get up. I wanted to sleep through to the following day when it would all be over.

Anxiety flowed through me; I had a job trial that night at a pub in North Melbourne. *I don't want the job. Why did I even apply? It'd been four weeks, plenty of time to heal enough to start work again, right?*

I had one more errand to run that day, so after pulling on the closest items of clothing I strolled towards the unfamiliar doctor's office, and it suddenly hit me how out of place I was. This wasn't my GP's surgery. I wasn't going for a consultation about an ear infection. I was going for a second Hepatitis-B vaccine because I might have had a disease.

I'm sick of this. Having to tell another person. Where do you start? Surely I should be a pro at this now, but it never gets easier to let those words slip out of my mouth.

What made it worse was that people greeted me with a bubbly work charm and asked me either how I was or what I needed, and I knew that I was about to slap that smile straight off their faces.

I walked through to the nurse's examination room, and the doctor who spoke to me briefly passed over his notes for the nurse to prepare my vaccination.

'Having it for a new job, or you off travelling?' a bubbly, heavy-set nurse asked.

'No, I was raped.'

And there it was. My ability to punch someone in the chest from the other side of the room. I didn't mean to, but how else do you say it? I tried saying it softly. Casually. Nothing pulls meaning away from those words.

She jabbed the needle gently into my left arm without breaking eye contact with me.

'Can I ask you for something? Can I hug you?' she asked once she had finished with my arm.

I nodded, and with that, she gave me a loving and gentle squeeze as she whispered in my ear, 'Please don't let this incident make you mistrust men.'

Our eyes connected, and instantly I knew we had shared the same experience. She had been hurt herself. She didn't have to say it, but I saw it in her eyes.

'Have you received any support yet, Alyshia?' the doctor asked me as he led me back into his consultation room while I pushed the small cotton ball hard against my arm where I had just been jabbed.

'I had a couple of phone calls with the crisis line, and I think they are trying to sort me out some face-to-face appointments soon.'

'Well, I want you to know that we offer counselling sessions here too. We have a great team, and I could arrange for an appointment for you if you would like that.'

I switched off before he made it to offering me an appointment. It wouldn't be free, and I knew exactly how much psychologists charge per hour.

'We might be able to get some of the costs covered, but not all of it,' he continued before I interrupted him.

'Thank you for that, but I really don't have much money. I think I'm going to wait and see when I get an appointment at the women's hospital.'

Thinking it was over, I reached down for my handbag as the friendly GP said, 'Well, listen, we are always here. If you need us, please, feel free to book another appointment. Even if you just need to talk.'

I thanked the doctor and made my way back home. The stress of the day was far from over. In fact, this was the easiest part of my day. The impending job trial kept my heart rate high. I wanted to pay my way more than anything, and after four weeks, I thought I was ready to give employment another try.

I scoured Gumtree, but I knew deep down that I wasn't ready for another bar position. I eventually came across a position for an events manager. Granted, it was in a bar/restaurant, but as long as I wasn't stuck behind a bar for too long, I knew I could do it.

My heart was pounding against my chest as Daniel drove me towards the pub. My trial was scheduled between 5 to 8pm. *I can't do this. Yes, Aly. Yes, you can. It won't happen again. You can do this.* I was told on the phone that I would be trialed on my ability to wait tables and serve behind the bar. Obviously just to see if I knew the fundamentals before giving me a higher position. *OK. I can do this.*

The entire drive there I wanted to scream *turn around!* Every stop at a traffic light was a relief. More time to breathe. *Maybe there will be diversions, and I'll be late for the trial. No point in going then, is there?*

Whenever I was anxious before, I would just tell myself how awesome I would be and how everything would be OK. This time was different. I had never had to convince myself so heavily that I could do something. For as long as I can remember, I have been my biggest critic. If I do something, I do it well. No half measures.

This time was different. I saw the pub in the distance, and my mind screamed for me to say something. We pulled up near the bar, and I hesitated. Daniel smiled and wished me good luck. I faked a smile and jumped out of the car.

'Just call me if you need me to come back earlier to pick you up, OK?' he said.

It was as if he could read my mind. Was *right now* too early?

I walked towards the bar. There was a queue. At least four people waiting. My fingertips went numb. Pins and needles coursed up my arms. *Where would Daniel be about now? Not far away. He could easily turn around.* I grabbed my phone and looked at the time. *I could just leave. Leave now. Have Daniel take me home.*

The person in front of me grabbed his pint and walked towards the seating area. I was up. *Fuck.*

The following two hours involved a rough thirty minutes of me looking like a deer caught in the headlights. An hour of sweaty palms and weak wrists, almost causing me to drop two plates piled high with chicken parmigiana and salad. It had rendered me useless at a job I knew like the back of my hand. I was stronger as a barmaid than a waitress, but I knew how to take orders and carry three plates. The large party of one-hundred people I was serving with a few other waitresses had dispersed, and looking down at my soft cloth while polishing cutlery, I honestly didn't care if I got the job.

I did it. I made it through. No panic attacks. I felt tense, sure, but I completed my trial.

The manager waved me over to the back of the bar. Again, I had very little interest in the outcome of this trial.

'You were fantastic, Aly! Good job! We definitely want to put you on the roster,' the small-duty manager said as he mulled over the crinkled roster hanging behind the bar.

I stood there in shock. *I was awful,* I thought to myself. Jesus. Trembling hands, fake smiles, near misses with an oversized parmy!

'Well?' Daniel asked as I flopped into the car, feeling utterly drained and exhausted.

'I got the job.'

'There y'go!' he beamed through tired eyes.

I had no intention of telling him how anxious it made me feel or how the thought of returning to work sent a spike of nausea through my entire body. I got the job. I could start earning some money. I just needed to wait for my stomach to return to its home under my ribs and I would be OK.

Chapter Twenty-Five

I Can't

I woke up with a huge knot in my stomach. My anxiety stemmed from the prospect of returning my black oversized work shirt to the Castle Hotel and telling them I could not take the job. I had never given up on anything in my life.

Every morning I woke, I had more anxiety than normal. A tight feeling deep within my gut kept reminding me I had to go to work soon. Back to a bar. Put a smile on, smarten yourself up and serve some drinks.

I've had a part-time job ever since I was thirteen, working in a fruit and vegetable shop. I loved to work, earn my own money, and pay my own way. But here I was being provided for at every turn. Not just food and a roof over my head, but opportunities to go out, buy clothes, have a coffee and a night out.

This made telling Daniel and his mom so much harder. I already felt like such a drain on them both emotionally and financially that I felt as though telling them was a slap in the face.

I couldn't do the job. I wasn't ready. Nowhere near ready. I wasn't just letting them down, I felt like I was letting myself down. Since arriving in Australia, I had never been refused a job after a trial. I could work behind any bar, no problem. Sure, I didn't know every cocktail, and I sometimes slipped in too much whisky when I was pouring. But I was quick, smiley and to be honest, really good at my job.

'Don't take the job, Aly,' Rita said, looking at me from her bedroom doorway.

'I'm scared,' I quietly said.

'No, no, no. You don't need to take it. Daniel and I are here. We can take care of you. It's way too soon. To be honest, when you told me you were going to a job trial I wanted to tell you to forget about it immediately. This could be a major setback for you, and you are doing so well. I just fear that someone, however innocently may touch your arm and you will freak out. I don't want that. You don't need that right now.'

Daniel drove me to North Melbourne, and I prayed that Nikki would be there, or at least James. Even though I had yet to meet James, he was the one who arranged the job trial for me over the phone.

I approached the bar to see Nikki's beaming smile. She was a petite woman with beautiful hair. I asked to speak to her in private. She looked worried and joined me around the other side.

'I can't take the job. I'm really sorry,' I mumbled as my face obviously screwed up.

'OK, that's fine. What's wrong?' her gentle voice spoke as an alarmed expression flashed quickly across her face

Then I told her. She stopped me halfway through my bumbling explanation and gently waved her arms at me.

'You don't have to explain. Don't feel bad. Oh God, hun. It's totally fine. It's not a problem at all.' Her arm went towards me but retracted back shapely.

'Can I give you a hug?'

'Yeah, sure.'

At that moment, this tiny, beautiful woman held me so tightly that I felt instantly at ease. With her face on my shoulder, she mumbled, 'You look after yourself. Take care of you. We are here if you need us. We aren't going anywhere, OK? Just know that.'

I had known Nikki for a total of three hours from the trial, but she already felt like a friend.

Before I handed back my shirt and left, she made me promise to stay out of the industry. She didn't want me around all the drunk punters, and after she discovered it was only five weeks since I'd been assaulted, she became insistent that I take a lot more time off.

Her eyes were full of concern that she attempted to mask with a smile.

As I walked back to the car, the anxiety lifted from my chest. I felt like falling onto the floor with relief.

This moment was short-lived.

Chapter Twenty-Six

The Art of Therapy

I called the emergency sexual assault helpline when I was at Daniel's. I knew I needed help. I had already called a hotline back in Western Australia one morning. I told them that I needed help and that I was open to it. I needed to talk, scream and cry to someone who wasn't in my inner circle. To have someone who was objective and outside of my world, looking in. Someone who wouldn't judge me or feel hurt, because believe me, I was not the only victim.

They said they would call me back and a counsellor would discuss what I needed and make a referral.

When she called me back, she asked me a lot of things. When did it happen? Did I report it? Has he been charged? Where did it happen? Where am I now? Am I safe? Who am I staying with?

As the incident happened so recently, they were very eager to get me an appointment as soon as possible. They informed me that they were short staffed, which I could understand given my background working in different health sectors. I didn't expect it to take over six weeks to be assigned my own counsellor, but I was happy to be given some sort of help in a country where I was not a citizen.

Queen Victoria Women's Hospital was smack in the centre of the city. They asked if I wanted to change location because I had to travel in from out near the airport. I said no. The bus ride was part of my healing. Facing people, the city. I knew that however hard it was going to be for me, it was for the best. I also knew that I could challenge myself while in the city to order a sandwich in a café or sit by the Yarra and have a glass of wine.

My therapy didn't end when I left that room. Every decision I made affected my recovery.

I decided to head into the city a couple of hours earlier than my appointment time, as I wanted to buy some paper and pens. Pinterest had become a great distraction for me as I scrolled through hundreds of drawings and easy-to-do patterns. They were so pretty. I had never been much of a doodler, but there was something about drawing that looked so therapeutic. Marking the blank paper with lines, dots and shapes required little thinking, and that was what I needed.

I headed into Big W, a huge department store in Australia, and walked straight towards the stationary section. That wasn't too scary. I just ignored everyone else around me and focused on picking out some supplies. Jumbo pack of Sharpies and an A4 art pad in tow, I headed out to find a coffee shop to begin my own therapy session before my appointment.

***

A well-built woman sat in the chair opposite mine. There was a small room with calming cream-painted walls, a small table with a clock facing the counsellor and a small window behind me. A session with little substance and just lots of note-taking.

Thinking back to the days where I wanted a job very similar to this, I found some strange annoyances that would really grind my gears. The small *hmm's* and *mmmmmm's*. After every sentence, there were sad eyes and *mmmm*.

Stop. Please. I know you are conveying sympathy, but it is just really annoying me. Just talk to me like a normal human being. Show sympathy, but not after every word I speak.

The hour went quickly. Surface details were discussed and whether I wanted to harm myself.

Back to the waiting game. I'd receive a call when a counsellor had a slot opening.

After the session was up, I wasn't ready to go back. The sun was shining, and I was starting to feel in control again. It's all about control. Power. Disabling a person's ability to control their situation. This loss of control lingered on for some time, but I felt a twinge. I wanted to stay in the city, around people. Not too many people, but some people. So I did.

I wandered down towards the Yarra and looked into the bars that stretched along the edge of the water. Melbourne is a beautiful city. Cosmopolitan, modern, cultural, everything you could want in one place.

I wonder if I could have a glass of wine and draw in my book. A question only two months ago would have sounded ridiculous. *Of course you can Aly. What's stopping you?* Something as simple as entering a bar alone for a drink left me crippled with anxiety. Frozen in fear. An act I wouldn't have thought twice about before became an unattainable goal.

I stared at the different establishments. There were so many people.

What about that one?

No, too expensive.

I turned my back and just sat on the grass bank. Next time. Next time, I will have a glass of wine by the water all by myself.

***

A few weeks passed before I was assigned my own counsellor. A petite woman with a warm smile popped her head around the door to the tiny waiting room.

'Alyshia?' she asked, smiling at me

'Yeah, sorry,' I apologised as I packed my drawing pad quickly into my bag.

I followed her slowly down a long white corridor with multiple small rooms jutting off here and there.

We talked, and near the end of the session, she asked how I found it.

'To be honest, I'd like to start next week by talking about some good things first. It just feels as though as soon as I sit down, even if I am feeling a little better, I have to start talking about deep and dark emotions. Can we start each session by talking about my week and positive stuff?' I bluntly requested.

'Of course we can! Absolutely. These are your sessions. I think that would be really good actually!' she chirped.

I knew from my background in the field that the counsellor would always tailor the session to the client. It always revolves around you, and the time you are appointed is yours to do with as you please. For me, I wanted to highlight the positive. Start the hour with what I had achieved. Whether it be eating at a café alone or being able to sleep without any medication.

The following week, Andrea did just that. We talked about how I went to a busy shopping centre by myself and how my morning anxiety attacks were slowly fading.

'It's strange y'no. I'm not afraid of men,' I started.

'Yeah?'

'Yeah. Men didn't do this to me. *One* man did this to me. Every man I pass on the street isn't a rapist. *He* was. I have absolutely no fear of the opposite sex in that way. Not saying I would feel comfortable with any guy flirting with me in a bar, but I don't hate them. I'm proud of myself.'

It was true. I was proud of myself. I was proud that my mind was stronger than I thought. I was making progress.

'How are the intrusive thoughts? Are you still getting them regularly?' she asked.

'Not as much. But when I do get them I try and just let myself feel as much as necessary,' I explained.

'What do you mean?' she pondered.

'Well, I allow myself to be upset. I know my mind needs to go through the motions. The anger, the sadness, the shame. I let it. If a thought comes into my mind, I allow it. I don't fight it. I cry if I need to cry. Then do something else. Move on. I move away from the thought, but I won't fight it.'

Andrea looked at me, completely stunned. There was a moment of silence.

'Aly, I need to be honest with you. I have never met anyone who is as strong headed as you are. You can tell you are very aware of yourself, and you are listening to your own body. Which is something most women I work with just won't do. They fight it all, and it makes them worse. But you, you're incredible, if you don't mind me saying.'

I'm not incredible. Far from it. I just want to get better.

For as long as I can remember, I have been praised for my strength and level-headedness. At that moment, I had no idea what strength really meant. How do you define strength after something like this? She reported it to the police? She didn't cry? She turned out just fine? I don't know. What made me able to find the strength to battle through this maze of horror?

I wasn't sure, but I am damn grateful for whatever it is.

I came to the conclusion that my underlying need to survive and being located 10,000 miles away from family and what used to be home intensified my situation. I had people around me, but in reality, I was alone. I was still in a country that wasn't my homeland. I still wanted to continue on with my life. I had a visa with an expiry date. I couldn't get comfortable or forget the world and hide under my duvet. I had to make myself better. I had no choice but to heal.

I was out in the wild, and if I didn't heal, life would move on without me. That scared me more than anything else did.

Chapter Twenty-Seven

YouTube

I was floating in between consciousness and REM when my body thrashed violently to open my eyes. They never opened. *You must open your eyes. Aly, please, open your eyes.* There was someone in the bed with me. Right next to me.

Aly, you have to open your eyes. My chest convulsed under my comatose body. *Wake up. He shouldn't be in your bed. He is going to hurt you.*

What is he doing here? How did he get here? Wake up Aly. You need to wake up. Run. Aly, run. He is going to hurt you. You have to run.

I bolted upright, but my lungs had collapsed in on themselves. I panted hard to try to breathe as I scanned the bed. My breathing slowed as I pulled myself up and cupped my head in my hands.

What have you done to me?

I had redeemed a morning routine since being in Melbourne. I swung my legs over the bed and headed into the kitchen. Filled the kettle. Clicked the button. Mug. Coffee. Sugar. Wait.

While waiting, my blood pressure would gradually climb. Water. Milk. Stir.

Sitting down on the stone step outside, I lit my cigarette. I had no interest in checking my email, video views or Facebook. I opened an app called Hotel Island. Intended for five-year-olds, clearly. You would build a hotel with different rooms and facilities on a pixilated interface. It was mundane. Distracting. Easy. It was everything I needed. I didn't need to read about tragedies happening across the world on my Facebook feed or stupid comments on my YouTube channel from trolls. I needed a simple distraction. Collecting coins and running my own online hotel.

A lot of repetitive tapping on the screen was surprisingly therapeutic.

I was glued to my phone as a distraction from the noise in my head. However, the days immediately following the incident, I couldn't bear to even pick up my phone. It was the furthest thing from what I wanted or needed. Being in the place I was, I didn't want to see what other people were doing. I didn't want to read messages from friends and subscribers asking how I was. So innocent; they had no idea. I pushed away from the online world with a tremendous force, as I knew it would be toxic to my healing.

After yet again clicking the 'clear notifications' button before reading a single one, I decided to make a short status on Facebook telling my subscribers that I wouldn't be online for a while.

I struggled with how to word it exactly. I didn't want friends and family to see it and worry. I didn't want phone calls demanding to know what was wrong. It had to be subtle. YouTube was never a job, and my audience wasn't that big, so who cared? Something along the lines of, *I'm busy, I need some time to relax and have fun. No need to worry.*

My phone buzzed beside me, notifying me that someone had commented on that status. I gulped hard and clicked. I was receiving such blind love. I smiled. Everyone telling me to take my time and that they hoped I was OK. That they would always be there when I was ready to return. These people didn't even know me and had no idea what had happened, yet they blindly supported me anyway. *Wow.*

Another thing that struck me was how aware I had become of my own issues. When no one else knows, you become hyper-alert. Every feeling is multiplied. It's true. A problem shared is a problem halved, but it's still your problem, and nothing can take that away.

It took me a while to get back into the idea of filming. I didn't want to upload for one reason. I didn't want to be fake. If I had filmed, I would have had to put on a big act, smile through the pain, and pretend that everything was OK. I'd prefer to lose every single subscriber than be someone I was not.

One morning felt different. My eyes welcomed the light glistening into my room with a strange sensation. Weightless. Calm.

I had begun to feel more and more like Aly every day. I had a way to go yet, but for once, I was optimistic.

I decided to film a video. Not because I had to, but because I had a strange urge to reconnect with complete strangers. Where I could just be me with people who didn't know, who didn't show pity when they looked at me. They wouldn't ask how I was or how I was coping because, to them, I was just a YouTuber who didn't upload for a while. It was everything I needed. My own form of therapy, yet no one knew.

I started to immerse myself back into a world of creativity and fun. Drawing was my tool when I didn't want to say a word, but now, I had words coming from everywhere!

Scott and I knew we had to cancel our plans to visit South East Asia, as my bank balance was plummeting. I felt so much guilt. He had his savings ready to go. We were so excited, but once again, I didn't have the money to do it.

New Zealand would come sooner than we liked, but it had to be done. Then my next concern—finding work. The idea of working with others petrified me. A single thought caused my anxiety to spike uncontrollably. My experience at the pub in Melbourne confirmed that I wasn't anywhere near ready to get back into an environment involving new faces and so much interaction.

But what else could I do? How on earth would I continue to travel now?

Then it happened.

In that instant, I realised that I had an incredible opportunity in front of me. Something I had wanted to do for so long, but had no idea how it was possible when I needed to work full-time to survive.

Now, with employment temporarily off the table for me to heal, I could take the plunge and make my therapeutic hobby into a career.

The problem was, I had no idea where to start. YouTube is fiercely competitive these days. Channels require years to grow a large enough audience to bring in enough dollars to sustain any lifestyle. I didn't have years. At this point, my channel was simply a hobby and nothing serious. After two years and a total of 10,000 subscribers, I was earning around $75 per month.

If other people can do this, why can't I? Why can't I be the success story? One of the minority who made it work.

All I had right now was time and a need to distract myself. I was in the perfect situation to make this work, and nothing would stop me from achieving my goal.

I don't believe that everything happens for a reason. I think that's a huge cop-out. X happens, and then Y happens. Correlation—not causation. X didn't necessarily cause Y to happen. As humans, we have a deep need to attribute meaning to absolutely everything in order to comfort ourselves. To find meaning in something tragic and horrible in order to make it not so bad. To make it seem as though it has some purpose.

Experiences have a lot of purpose after they occur, not before. X did not happen with the conscious intention of Y being an awesome outcome. No. Y happened because it happened. If Y is good, great! Happy days. However, for some reason, it is so hard for people to accept that something bad can happen for no good reason.

That's what happened to me. I lived through trauma that no person should have to experience. For no reason other than a sick individual decided that if he didn't get what he wanted, he was going to take it through force. There was no reason for this to happen to me.

Believing that everything happens for a reason takes away the power of the human spirit. Why not say, 'X happened, so *I* did this despite it causing me pain.' Pat yourself on the back. Stop handing over this 'coincidental alternative success' to something else. God. The universe. No. When something bad happens, *you* and only *you* can decide what happens next.

You didn't decide for your boss to go bankrupt, but you can decide how you will react to it and move forward. You didn't decide to let your house burn down due to faulty electrical work. However, you decide whether you pick up those pieces while looking back or looking forward.

I was taking the next step in my life. I took a bad situation and pulled out the positive. You could say, 'Why didn't you just decide to go back to work? Like you said, you decide how you react.'

You're right. At the time, my anxiety attacks were overwhelming. If YouTube wasn't an option, I would have indeed put that strength into dealing with my anxiety. Instead, I killed two birds with one stone and did both.

When a person is sexually assaulted, one of the most common immediate responses is shock. Not shock in the way that most of us experience regularly, for instance, when we watch the latest celebrity scandal on the news. But full body shock, which is a completely physiological response to a traumatic experience. The mind immediately triggers our fight or flight response. Like a gazelle spotting a lion, you can freeze, fight or run. Our brains are so hardwired and so good at what they have been doing for so many years that this decision isn't a conscious one. Your brain is old and experienced.

Thousands of years of lessons learnt have been passed down through your genes for that moment.

The decision of what to do next has already been decided, and your conscious self is no longer a player. Your basal instinct is to survive. Your brain will not let you mess up by interfering.

Shock is your brain's way of protecting you. When an event is so damaging, so traumatic and so psychologically harmful, your brain turns off. It shuts down. Imagine a small worker in your head running around and switching off departments in your brain. Emotional response? Off. Thought processes? Nope. Short-term memory retrieval? Smashed and selective. Alertness? Only to survival, nothing else. Anger? Gone. Pain? Gone. Sadness, envy, humour are all disabled. Your brain needs to conserve energy. Your basal instances are on high alert and not much else.

It's different for everyone, but how long this numbness lasts varies. It lasts however long your brain needs it to last. Again, you are not in control. This whole experience has centred on a lack of control. From the moment the event occurred, right up until you lash out twelve months later when something triggers you. The most critical element to try to rebuild is control.

As I sat looking at my YouTube dashboard, I felt in control. Real control. For the first time in weeks. I was the boss.

Being the boss, I opened a new tab and typed in 'How to build Subscribers on YouTube' followed by 'How to make money on YouTube'.

As the weeks progressed, my search became more detailed. Marketing techniques. Increasing engagement. SEO optimisation. Website design. WordPress plugins. Social media techniques. Photography. Lighting. YouTube searchability.

There would always be a backup plan. Finding a 9 to 5 in New Zealand. I would have Scott. That would always be an option, but in reality, the only option I ever present to myself when I want something is success. If I want something, I get it. I'll work hard for it. I'll make mistakes. I'll get better. There are no excuses. If others could do this, so could I. It's not fairy dust; it's hard work, and that was something I wasn't afraid of.

***

Before I could begin on the long road towards online success, I still had a lot of personal growth to cover. I realised that I hadn't gone shopping in some time. Sure, I had visited the local second-hand stores but nothing more. I rarely bought anything new, but I always loved perusing shopping centres and rooting around in the bargain bins. I grabbed my Myki card and headed out.

As I entered, I noticed mothers barging past me with plastic bags hung from the handles of their pushchairs, pained looks on their faces as they raced to catch their bus. Young teens hung around the small leather stools chatting with each other. No one batted an eyelid at me. There was no reason for me to be afraid here. *No one here will hurt me. I am just another person in this huge crowd.* I found a certain comfort in that. Just another face.

I decided to lift my head when I realised I was staring at my feet, and a shop front caught my eye. Colette was a large, trendy bag shop in Australia, but their style had never appealed to me. In amongst the various handbags and scattered fairy lights was a white clutch bag with a thin gold chain that stopped me in my tracks.

Across the front read 'off-duty blogger'.

That was my bag. Without a thought, I walked straight in, picked it up from the mirrored shelf and proceeded to the counter.

I don't believe in signs, but how often do you come across anything related to bloggers? It felt as though my previous epiphany to take my online hobby full-time was confirmed with nothing more than a handbag.

I didn't just feel in control—I felt empowered. *That's right world. I'm a blogger. Just look at my bag if you don't believe me!*

With a newfound sense of exhilaration that I knew probably wouldn't last, I decided to take my new bag out on a date. Down to a bar on the Yarra for a glass of wine.

In typical Melbourne fashion, the blue skies were engulfed in grey clouds, and the heavens opened over the city. I didn't care! The pub had tables with large parasols. I'd be fine.

Daniel was working a shift at the NGV (National Gallery of Victoria), not far from my chosen bar. I ordered the cheapest glass of Shiraz and found a seat under an umbrella. The place was entirely empty. Drinks at waterside establishments are best under the warming sun. But not for me. This was perfect.

Chapter Twenty-Eight

Home

I am in the depths of North Korea. I am with someone. A Man. We are in trouble. We have a house, but they found us and got through the boarded-up windows. I go to a caravan to stay with a family, but I can't tell them all about it. I know the family, but I can't really tell them everything. I am messaging Daniel in code. I can't type exactly what is happening, so it takes a long time to get the message through. I sit looking out of where the window used to be in the caravan. A man dragged me out. I tried to talk him down. He was looking for me. He had a Stanley blade in his hand and tried to chop my fingers off. He was on top of me, and I was fighting him off, looking at the blade coming closer to my thumb. I ran back inside and told them. They were totally shocked but soon returned to their business.

I left the caravan and ran. A slow forced run. Hooligans were everywhere. Groups of teenagers with petrol bombs. I dodged them. Some caught me, but I managed to keep running.

At no point during this event did I want to run home. It was nothing personal to my family, but I just didn't feel the need. I knew they would be supportive and loving. They would have probably flown to Australia to bury the bastard 6ft under. But for some reason, going home never entered my head. It wasn't travelling that did this to me.

Perhaps that was what I was scared of, being told at the age of twenty-four that I had to stop travelling. Travelling was too dangerous. See. Look what happened.

The truth of the matter is, I could have been raped anywhere. In my own room at the home I lived in for the first seventeen years of my life. Down my street. In the car park of my local pub. In fact, that was more likely. It wasn't because I was travelling that this happened. This could have happened anywhere at any time.

I suppose, in a way, I was scared of the idea of people caring for me. I was scared of hurting them. I knew it would break my parent's hearts knowing what happened to me; that they would forever blame themselves for not being there. When in reality, they could never protect me from something so heinous.

From a young age, I have witnessed my parents face pain and suffering. Unhappiness. Divorce. Resentment. I have been independent from a young age. For as long as I can remember, I wanted to protect them. Crazy I know; a child should never feel the need to protect their parents, but I have always had the overwhelming urge to do so.

I knew how much I meant to them. Putting myself in their shoes, I always thought, *How would I feel if my child came to me and told me this happened to them?* I'd be heartbroken and angry.

At this point, I didn't want to have to explain what had happened. Time had passed. My statement was given. Charges were pressed. I didn't want to have to start again and tell them from the beginning. Of course, they'd want to know, but I was moving forward. I was looking to the future, taking steps towards healing and leaving the past in the past. I didn't need it brought up again and again.

How else would I tell them? Hey, I was sexually assaulted, but I don't want to tell you any details or discuss anything right now.

Is he being charged? When is it going to court? Who is he? Where are you? Get home now. Are you safe? Why didn't you tell us earlier? I told you travel could be dangerous!

I understand why people don't want to report sexual assault. After being violated in the most despicable way possible, being degraded, demeaned and raped, the last thing people want to do is talk about it while spreading their legs for strangers in a cold hospital room.

Before my world was flipped upside down, I could see my path laid out in front of me. I could see the bustling markets of downtown Bangkok. The steaming pho served street-side in Vietnam.

I stood looking down on an empty pathway, one that I needed to pave myself. When I set out for

Australia, I expected to learn more about myself than ever before and discover new things that I loved and equally things that I hated. I thought I would meet people who would shape my life in unimaginable ways.

My time in Melbourne was quickly coming to an end. I had a flight back home that I booked back when I thought it would be a good idea to touch base; before that night stole a small part of me.

Even though the path I had to take to get where I am now was unforeseen, I still took it.

PART THREE

Chapter Twenty-Nine

Court

'Just tell your story. Remember, you are not the one on trial, even though his defence lawyer will make you feel that way. It is going to be really tough, Aly.'

The words from the prosecutor boomed in my head as I sat at the end of a long table at a conference room in Auckland, talking to a camera linked back to Australia. That's how it would be done. They discussed flying me out to stand in court, or really, a safe room within the courthouse. I didn't want that. I'd be alone. We couldn't afford to pay for Scott's ticket, so I would have no one at my side.

Instead, it was set that I would present my side via a live video link from Queenstown. Scott and I arrived at our hostel three days before the court date. We had been travelling around New Zealand for over six months up until this point, the whole time I was trying to forget everything that had happened in Western Australia. I was told I would have a court support worker there by my side at all times. Someone who had been through this procedure multiple times before and could be a steady hand for me.

With the time difference, I arrived at the school around midday, keeping my head down and working my way through the Kiwi kids towards the conference room. We went through what I would see on screen, how everything would play out and some techniques to keep calm if I became overwhelmed.

I was told to read my statements again, print them out, and have them in front of me when I appeared in court. I wouldn't be allowed to look at the statements unless it was absolutely necessary. I had to remember the evening that I had pushed away so hard for so long. The event that I put in a box and buried within my mind had to be pulled out and looked at again. I had spent so much time moving on with my life and surrendering the details to the past, and those details were now going to be in the forefront of my mind once again.

The incident itself was the most traumatic. Reliving it in detail was second. Given the fact that I was not the one on trial and it wasn't me who was being judged, I was about to spend multiple hours being told that I was a liar. What angle the defence would take was unknown. Would they paint me as a gold digger? A slut? It didn't matter. After everything that had happened, I would have to sit there and defend myself.

The most sickening aspect of all of it—he didn't even have to stand and give evidence at the trial. The justice system says that you are innocent until proven guilty. It was my job to prove he was guilty. If he decided, he could sit back and relax. I understood this, and in all honesty, that is how the justice system should work. It is there to protect the innocent. But what if they are not innocent? What happens when you try to prove that an individual committed one of the most horrific crimes when there is only one word against the other?

By this point, it wasn't all about getting the extremely unlikely verdict of guilty. It was about telling my story. It was holding a monster accountable. It was about me having my day in court.

The prosecutor explained how the day would play out. First, I would be questioned by the state prosecutor (the one on my side) who would gently lead me through the series of events in order for me to tell my story to the jury. Then, after a break, I would be questioned by the defence (on his side). This is the part that is most traumatic for the victim. Defence lawyers will use brutal tactics to make you feel like you are the one on trial. Like you were guilty and wrong. That you are a dirty little liar. If you dare stumble over a word, they will jump on you, twist it and show the jury that you are clearly lying.

I knew it was going to be brutal. Horrific. Long. I knew they would pull every minute detail and question it. They would take a simple statement or question such as 'Why did you let him buy you a drink?' And make you look bad for doing something as innocent as having a drink with a potential boss. They make you panic, twisting the events so strategically that while you are verging on a panic attack, your mind is flooded with flashbacks, they will make you stumble and second-guess yourself. Sure, the judge and prosecutor are there to protect you from the defence breaking the rules and pushing you too far; but they are so good, sometimes the judge doesn't even notice.

The video link would take place in a local school in Queenstown, New Zealand. A large room with a wide screen, a table and two chairs. The support worker assigned to my case was a small lady who spoke very softly. She would be there for me and walk me through ways in that I could handle my emotions when being questioned.

She held her ID badge up to the camera and stated her name and occupation to the court before sitting back by my side. My heart was racing. I couldn't count the beats fast enough, as it felt like my heart was thumping in my throat.

The judge was on screen, donning a black gown, short grey hair and an aged face. At no point would I see the jury. Only the judge, the prosecutor and the defence.

Evan, the prosecutor, appeared on screen. A young, tall man with very short hair.

Long deep breaths, Aly. He is on your side. Just take your time and tell your story.

As imagined, Evan led me through the events of that night without pushing me or triggering me. He made sure I covered important details by leading me through my story slowly and precisely. That was the easy part. I kept breathing. My heart wouldn't slow. This was only easy compared to what I was about to face. His defence.

After a short break, I was called back into the room. With the time difference between New Zealand and Western Australia, the sun had already set on my end, the darkness mirroring the sinking feeling in my chest.

My eyes widened, and my heart stopped when the camera switched to his defence lawyer, a woman. Her hair was frizzy and out of control. Her face was the polar opposite to Evan's, stern and cold. She began her questioning.

Before you give your evidence, it's explained to you by the prosecutor and the court support worker that it is more than OK to say, 'I don't know,' or 'I can't remember.' The court is very aware that rape trials reach the courtroom months or even years after the event occurs. You are not expected to remember every single detail. Especially when you have purposefully buried the event deep inside of yourself for so long.

Without me, there wouldn't be a court case. Without my evidence, it would all be for nothing. This pressure built up inside of me every day leading up to the court date.

'I feel as though it's my job to prove that he is guilty,' I said to Evan over the phone a few days before court.

'No, Alyshia. That's my job. Look, I have been trained for years to do just that. I am the one who needs to prove to the jury that he is guilty. Not you. You just tell your story the best you can—I will do the rest.'

***

I sat fingering a plush Elmo toy in my hands, taking long, deep breaths.

The defence began by throwing me a curveball. She had a pile of documents in front of her that she combed through one by one.

'I see you write blogs under the website psycho traveller dot com, is that correct?' she stated.

My face dropped. *What?* What does that have to do with any of this? Where was she going with all this?

'Yes, I do,' I answered.

'You tell people that they can travel the world and it can be cheap. You write a lot about getting things for free. You seem to have quite the obsession with it actually. Taking free samples from hotel rooms and the like. Is that true?' She looked up at me, glaring.

'Yes, I show people how to travel on a budget,' I replied, completely stunned.

A traveller with little money and a rich soon-to-be boss who she could sleep with for a raise. That was the angle she was taking.

'I also see you have a Patreon page where people can give you money for doing absolutely nothing. Is that correct? You like to take money from people to do absolutely nothing?'

'No. That is not correct. I have a Patreon page for people to support me in producing content online, which is work,' I said, with probably too much sass.

That pile of papers were printouts from my blog, Facebook page and Twitter account. Anytime I mentioned money or getting something for free, it was pulled out and used as evidence of me being a cheap little gold digger who would do anything for cash.

I answered her questions about the night's events as best I could. She tried to twist my statement and words, but it didn't work. I answered calmly and honestly. If I couldn't remember a tiny detail, I said, 'I do not remember.' The thing is, the defence will try to make you trip over your own words. However truthful your words are, it is their job to make it look like something it isn't.

Was the fourth drink purchased by you or him? Was the fifth drink in a small or large glass? If you try and guess what you *think* is correct, the chances are they will run with your confused state, magnify it and show the jury just how unreliable your story is. Yes, even a tiny detail like the shape of a glass or the exact time you had your second drink will be used against you if you cannot recall it perfectly. It's what they are trained to do.

His defence was so good at what she was doing; she caused me to have a full-on panic attack.

Up until that point, I was silently proud of myself for how I was handling the experience. I remembered to breathe, answering the most difficult questions with ease and calm. I felt confident. I told my story. I squeezed my Elmo as hard as I needed and knew it would all be over soon.

She asked me about a detail I amended in my statement. I knew this question was coming. My heart began to race. I couldn't remember what part of the statement she was referring to. I had zoned out due to shock.

'I'm not sure exactly which statement it's in,' I said.

'She doesn't know,' she said, addressing the jury before turning back to me. 'Well, surely you would know. Did you say it or didn't you?'

'I'm not sure whether it was in my original statement or if I added it to a later statement.' I stated, my heart pounding harder—if that was even possible.

She started snarling at me, raising her upper lip, a wicked smile fluttering around her mouth. She held up a copy of my statement to the camera.

'This is your statement Alyshia, correct?'

'Yes.'

'Then I really don't see why you have such a problem telling us what time you ordered the drink and whether you put the information into your first or second statement.' Her eyes were piercing through the camera lens. She latched onto my lapse in memory, and I could see she wasn't going to let it go.

My chest began to hurt.

Breathe Aly.

'I cannot remember exactly whether I said that in my first or second statement. If I could look then I would be able to tell you,' I said, as my lips started trembling uncontrollably.

The court doesn't want the victim to look at the statement for many reasons. The obvious one is to ensure you can be questioned fairly, which was fine. But another is because it can upset the victim, having to comb through the statement again.

She wouldn't let this drop, addressing me one second and then using my increased panic against me when addressing the jury next.

'I'm sorry. I can't remember which statement I said it in-'

'Why can't you remember? This is very simple. Would the court allow Miss Ford to check her statement? She clearly needs help.'

I started to hyperventilate. The judge, prosecutor and defence started talking amongst themselves, discussing whether she should drop it and move on or let me look at my statement. This detail was insignificant to the grand scheme of things, but looking back, I know she did this on purpose. I had been so calm answering her questions that she needed to trip me up and make me flustered, and it worked.

'I'm sorry, I'm sorry, I can't remember.' Tears started to roll down my cheeks as I gasped for air.

'Miss Ford, please take a break for a moment and get some air. Come back when you are ready,' the judge ordered.

I walked to the back of the room, opened the door and collapsed into Scott's arms. Sobbing hard, he stroked my back, trying to get my breathing back under control.

'Miss Ford, please retrieve the copy of your statement in front of you,' the judge requested when I re-entered the room.

'Page five, about halfway down,' the defence directed me. 'Now can you answer me?'

'Yes, that is correct, what I said,' I confirmed after reading a line of my statement.

The defence exhaled long and hard, as if my inability to remember every tiny detail exhausted her.

She finally moved on after causing me to have a panic attack, leave the room and then look at my statement. She did it to paint a picture of a bumbling liar.

Once the defence finishes asking their questions, the prosecutor has the chance to come back one more time. You see, his lawyer, like I said earlier, would be sneaky and cut me off before I had finished answering. Technically, they are not allowed to do this, but things are missed by the judge.

Evan's words to me days before the trial ran through my head. *I have your back in there. She'll cut you up, and if the judge doesn't notice, I can object or bring it up at the end and give you time to say what you wanted to say. Also, if I want anything clarified, that's when I will bring it up.*

Evan did come back at the end with a few questions. He wanted me to be able to finish what I was saying about victim compensation, something I wasn't even thinking about. The defence brought it up in an attempt to show that all I wanted was money. I interjected to say that she was wrong, but she moved on before the judge had noticed. Luckily, Evan noticed and gave me a platform to talk, uninterrupted.

'That will be all Miss Ford. We won't need anything more from you,' the judge said, gesturing to someone to terminate the call.

As I stepped out of the room and the call cut out, I fell into Scott's arms and let out a long, high-pitched groan. It was over. Relief swept over my entire body, forcing a laugh up my throat.

It's over. I did it. It's done.

Oh my God. It's finally fucking over.

Chapter Thirty

Verdict

It started to matter less and less what that verdict would be. The anxiety and the tears, the fear and the anticipation, having my day in court and telling my story freed me from the cage that surrounded me since it all happened. No matter what happened next, the truth was out there, and I felt so liberated.

It would be a few days before I heard the verdict, so we packed up our things and continued our New Zealand road trip. The trial was not going to take away my ability to live my life.

As I sat editing a new video in our hostel in Wanaka, my phone started to ring. Unknown number. I picked up the phone, walked into our room and closed the door before answering.

'Hi Alyshia, how have you been?' Evan asked, so calmly that I couldn't read his emotions.

'I'm OK, just on a bit of a road trip to clear my head.'

'Good. OK. It was a unanimous verdict amongst the jury. He was found not guilty.'

Over the past year, I was told by every police officer, detective, counsellor and prosecutor to expect a not guilty verdict on a case like this. Still, my entire body slumped onto the bed with an air of defeat.

'The jury believed you...' he started.

What? But I thought you just said —

'The problem is as we discussed before, they have to be *more* than sure that he did it. If they get it wrong, they are putting a man with a family in jail for a major crime. They have to be sure. They actually didn't like him at all. He kept glaring at the jury so much they sent a note to the judge saying that he made them feel uncomfortable,' he continued.

'What about the tampon?' I asked. The only hard piece of evidence we had that I never consented.

'It was brought up, of course. But his defence presented the idea to the jury that because you had been drinking, you could have forgotten to remove it.'

Of course. I know so many women who 'forget'.

'The evidence may have tipped the verdict if there was no alcohol involved. Alyshia, it's an all-too-common tale. Drinking is not illegal; but the moment alcohol is presented into the mix, the jury will not hesitate to lean away from a guilty plea. It's wrong, but the jury is just being careful. They have to make the decision that the evidence proves beyond reasonable doubt. Unfortunately, that causes most of these cases to slip through the cracks.'

There was a long pause.

'I know this probably won't mean much, but he lost the $50,000 cash deposit on the pub, and the sale fell through.'

'Yeah, thanks, but it doesn't mean much,' I stated.

The verdict neither shocked me nor upset me. From the hospital room right up until now, I had expected those two words. For me, this whole process was about letting go of the pain. Ironically, the process amplified and induced so much pain that it was unbearable. Within hours of being violated, I was sat in a cold room for seven hours, asked to take off my dress before it was placed in an evidence bag, and asked to open my legs a little bit wider. I was stuck with so many needles and had to swallow so many pills, all with a complete stranger sitting next to me. In the months following those seven hours, I endured flashbacks, panic attacks, depression, anxiety, disgust, and anger.

Once all this had passed and life started to get brighter and more positive, I had to relive it all again. The evening. The drinks. What I was wearing. What he was wearing. The court process. Managing my emotions. Anger. Pain. Panic. Anxiety.

From the moment I dialled those three numbers to my final words in court, I had to constantly remind myself why I was doing it. When someone so despicable and evil does something so heinous, they must be stopped. They have to be held accountable. If not by the victim, then who? Who else can bring monsters like that to justice? The person they have hurt the most. You.

The moment I muttered 'thank you' to the judge and stepped outside of the conference room in New Zealand, relief flooded through my body, from the tips of my toes to the end of my long hair. That moment was the most liberated I have ever felt in my entire life. I was so happy that I laughed.

Most acts of sexual assault go unreported. Through fear or shame, the victim retreats away from the event. I get it. I completely get it. But these individuals will most likely do it again. To someone else. Again and again. Each victim not reporting it. Each time, the monster's power grows stronger, and they feel more invincible.

I am not going to tell you that reporting it is easy. You should have read enough by now to know that it's traumatic and testing. But it needs to be done. These monsters need their power taken away from them by the people they have hurt.

Because if not you, then who?

-END-

Epilogue

I started piecing together stories for a possible book when I was on the sheep station in Queensland. There were so many crazy new experiences that I thought would make an interesting read. I never really took the book seriously; I just stitched together moments to see how it would turn out.

After the incident, I started to write my thoughts down in order to cope with what had happened. It was on one cloudy day that I looked at my writing and thought, *Should this go into my book?* At the time, I had no idea what to do with all of those pieces. I certainly wasn't in the right frame of mind to tell the world. Hell, even my nearest and dearest didn't know what happened. I just kept writing and writing, and the book you are holding started to take shape. These pages are my therapy.

When Scott and I arrived in New Zealand, he picked up work pretty quickly as an electrician. Deep down inside I knew I wanted to make a full-time income from YouTube and my blog, but that would require me to give it my full attention.

Three days after arriving in Auckland, I received a message from a language learning company who wanted to be a regular sponsor on my channel. After taking a couple of lessons, I decided to agree and signed a contract whereby I would feature them twice a week. The money

I received was a beacon of hope, but not enough to support me fully.

'Just do it,' Scott said.

'But we need more money. I can't rely on you to help me with the rest,' I said, bowing my head, feeling as though my path was about to crumble.

'Look, I don't know how I know this, but your channel is going to be huge. I have no doubt you will be successful. Look at how much you have grown so far. Seriously, Aly, you have to do this. Don't worry about the money. You cannot let this opportunity slip away.'

From that moment, I stuck my head into every article, tutorial, and book I could find about building an online business. Since I committed to making travel my lifestyle and turned my online content into a sustainable income stream, I have visited many countries around the world. From Hong Kong to Thailand to Mauritius. I finally got to eat pho in Vietnam and witness the sunrise over Angkor Wat.

Life knocked me down, and it took my dreams, plans and future with it. In return, it left me with a new dream. It left me with the 'something else' I originally left the UK to find.

Even as I am sat writing this, an unbelievable amount of fear and doubt around publishing this book lies deep within my gut. Being a figure on the internet with over 180,000 people waiting to see my next move; it is terrifying to put this part of my life out there.

So why have I?

During a break I had between being questioned by the prosecutor and hounded by the defence, I spoke with my court support worker.

'Do you get many foreigners who have to do a video link?' I asked, just to fill the silence.

'Oh yes! Way more than you can imagine. I have had a lot of young travellers here with a similar experience to yours.' Her words flew out of her mouth like a missile heading straight towards my heart.

I swallowed hard. *Oh my God.*

Up until this point, I had been plagued by doubt and fear. Every word I wrote of this book brought me closer to sharing my story. But right there at that moment, it dawned on me that this wasn't just *my* story. This was a story shared by millions. Dialling those three numbers was as much for me as it was for every other man and woman out there who never found the strength to do it.

This book is as much for you as it is for me. It's for every single person who has been, or might be, hurt. For everyone who loses themselves completely, and continues to fight their battle to discover a way to move on. This is my story. This is your story. This is *our* story.

You see the thing is, before this book was published, only a handful of people knew about what happened to me. It's not something you bring up over a beer at your hostel. It made me look at people in a completely different way. Meeting me, you may never guess this had ever happened.

How many young men and women are walking around holding onto this secret? Are they ashamed? Scared? Were they thousands of miles from home with no one to run to for help? Did they just run away, not report it to the foreign police, and just forget about it? Wouldn't you?

My heart felt like it was about to explode. What if I had no one to run to when this happened to me? What if I didn't have Shaz, Daniel, Rita and Scott? Would I have just run away from it? Would I have made an excuse, packed my bags and jumped on the next bus out of there?

I called the police that night, because not only was it the right thing to do, but also because somewhere inside of me, I knew I was strong enough to handle it.

You see, the fact that the conviction rate is so low on sexual assault cases, along with the traumatic process the victim must go through to get the predator charged at the least, puts women off even bothering. *What's the point?* They tell themselves. *They won't get charged anyway, and I have already just gone through hell!* This is what I was told by the detective and a police officer.

If you do not report a crime, then this person will walk around with a clean record. Not just a criminal record but also a local police record. However, if you report it, even if he walks free later on, there will always be a mark on his record. Therefore, if this happens again, the police can look at their records and see that this is not the first time this person has been accused of this crime.

A single event by a single person is not enough for me to stop living the life I want. An event that could have happened to anyone. An event that was never foreseen. These events on any level, whether they be horrific, violent, financially crippling or emotionally draining, are events that can happen to anyone. The only thing you have control over is what you do next. How you use what has happened.

When life knocks you back, you'll believe that it has also taken your control. The reality is that it hasn't taken control of your life. It has only taken your belief that you still have it. It hides it deep within yourself. It's a long, hard journey to find it again. It's about whether you decide to go and look for it or give up.

Sometimes there are singular moments in life that change everything: your outlook, your relationships, your self-esteem, and your self-worth. These events shove you into a dark abyss while you close the lid on it, or you can fight your way back up, growing stronger with every step, learning with each stride so by the time you reach the light you are armed with an arsenal of lessons and are ready to take on the world.

This has been my journey—a journey that began and ended with so many dreams, hopes, desires and ambitions. A journey of the ultimate highs and most catastrophic lows. A journey no one could ever write about before it happened. A journey that has left me on the other side, a completely different version of myself.

Five years ago, Aly was a bright and optimistic twenty-two year old. She had a bumpy ride throughout those years and emerged victorious time and time again. She decided to challenge the path in front of her. For her, life was all about risk. She knew by taking a chance, she would ultimately learn something. Whether psychology was her true calling and a life of study was the path meant for her, or whether she would discover something else. Another occupation. Even if she didn't, Aly was happy just to take the chance and have fun.

The Aly from five years ago never left England on a journey of self-discovery. She found the thought of trying to find herself in South East Asia too much of a cliché to stomach. She left because curiosity got the better of her. She left because she feared regret more than anything.

As I stand here today, forcing myself to look back on the journey that she took, I feel an overwhelming sense of pride. I speak of myself in the third person because the Aly who existed back then is not the Aly I am today. I have evolved and grown in so many unexpected ways.

I thought that my anxiety towards working in a bar and being so far from home was what pushed me towards the life I have right now. I was wrong. The anxiety was simply a catalyst; my fear of regret and overwhelming curiosity grew within me. I took the chance. I grabbed the opportunity that lay in front of me with both hands. Whether I sank or swam, this door would not remain open for long. If I didn't run through it and risk falling into the abyss on the other end, I wouldn't be here writing this book.

On the other side of the door were mountains of obstacles and directions in a language I couldn't understand; doubt and fear were everywhere. I had very little money and zero experience. To begin with, the only thing that kept me moving forward was occasionally looking back. Because looking back, I saw absolutely nothing. I sprinted through the door and slammed it behind me. I stood on a path that began at my feet. It reminded me that if there is no way back, the only way is forward.

Your path may lead you to a door one day. Perhaps it already has once or twice. When there is a loaded truck hauling behind you at full force, you may have only a moment to decide whether to jump at the opportunity before it passes you by. The force pushing me from behind was a monster. It spewed out nasty words, determined to take me down a long, dark, winding path, in a direction that terrified me.

My life now is unforeseen and certainly not perfect, but it's a life I created for myself, against all the odds. I gave myself the gift of freedom and independence. My home is wherever there is a decent Wi-Fi connection and soft sand. I am my own boss. I move when I feel like it and work when it suits me. Sure, I can bash out seventy-hour weeks like any young and eager entrepreneur, but it's my choice.

I could look back and wonder for hours where I would be if that night hadn't occurred, but it would be pointless. I can look back on Australia and not feel hurt or angry. I look back and see all the friends I made and the incredible experiences I had, even those in that tiny Outback town in Western Australia. It's just another chapter in my life—a long and gruelling chapter that I thought would never end.

From it, I took what I could and held my head high. I will treasure each and every memory I created in Australia. Good or bad, these series of events led me to where I am today. How on earth could I be mad about that?

About the Author

Born in Birmingham, Aly always had a strong desire to help others in need. During her studies at the University of Glamorgan, she put her head down for three years with the dream of completing her clinical doctorate one day in the future. However, her love of travel and curiosity to discover the unknown led her to put everything on hold to see what was out there.

Since then, her adventures have taken her across five continents and into the heart of over thirty countries, documenting every step, while bashing misconceptions and showing the reality of life on the road. Through her battle to make a career on a crowded online platform, Aly isn't afraid of showing her followers the ups and downs of nomadic life.

Follow Aly's adventures across the globe here:

YouTube: http://www.youtube.com/psychotraveller

Blog: http://www.psychotraveller.com

Social Media

Facebook: https://www.facebook.com/psychotraveller

Twitter: https://www.twitter.com/psychotraveller

Instagram: https://www.instagram.com/psychotraveller

If you have been a victim of sexual assault, please contact the police as soon as you are safe. If you or someone you know has been affected by sexual assault, please reach out to the following people for help:

Europe

Children

Rape Crisis England and Wales
 https://rapecrisis.org.uk/
 Helpline: 0808 802 9999

Rape Crisis Scotland
 https://www.rapecrisisscotland.org.uk/
 Helpline: 08088 01 03 02

Victim Support
 https://www.victimsupport.org.uk/crime-info/types-crime/rape-and-sexual-assault
 Helpline: 0808 168 9111

Survivors UK - Male rape and sexual abuse
 https://www.survivorsuk.org/

Rape Crisis Network Europe
 https://www.rcne.com/

Australia

Reachout
https://au.reachout.com/articles/sexual-assault-support

National Sexual Assault Support Helpline: 1800 737 732

New Zealand

HELP

http://helpauckland.org.nz/

HELPline: 09 623 1700

USA

RAINN

https://www.rainn.org/

Helpline: 800 656 4673

Canada

Ending Violence Association of Canada

http://endingviolencecanada.org/getting-help/

Please visit the website above for a helpline within your area.

Asia

International Directory of Domestic Violence Agencies

http://www.hotpeachpages.net/asia/index.html

92563771R00149

Made in the USA
Middletown, DE
09 October 2018